PARAMHANSA SWAMI YOGANANDA

[The following dates are written in English in the original Bengali manuscript. The author was showing the time period during which the book was written.]

October 1983–4th January 1984

Yoga Niketan

www.yoganiketan.net

email: yoganiketan@yoganiketan.net

surface mail contact:

Yoga Niketan
167 Swakeleys Road
Ickenham
Middlesex
London
UB10 8DN
United Kingdom

PARAMHANSA SWAMI YOGANANDA

Life-portrait and Reminiscences

Sri Sailendra Bejoy Dasgupta

English translation by Yoga Niketan

iUniverse, Inc.

New York   Bloomington

PARAMHANSA SWAMI YOGANANDA
Life-portrait and Reminiscences

iUniverse books may be ordered through booksellers or by contacting:

iUniverse
1663 Liberty Drive
Bloomington, IN 47403
www.iuniverse.com
1-800-Authors (1-800-288-4677)

Because of the dynamic nature of the Internet, any Web addresses or links contained in this book may have changed since publication and may no longer be valid. The views expressed in this work are solely those of the author and do not necessarily reflect the views of the publisher, and the publisher hereby disclaims any responsibility for them.

Printed in the United States of America

iUniverse rev. date: 07/14/09

Contents

[The following images are scans of the original Bengali manuscript]

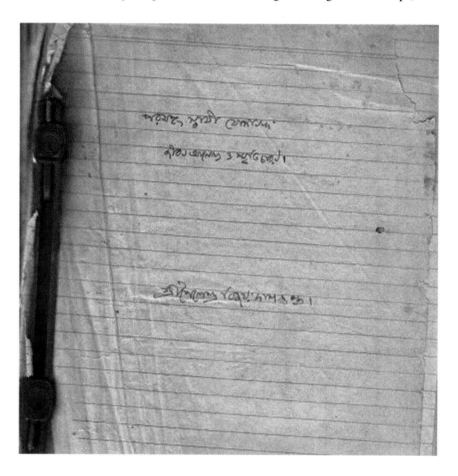

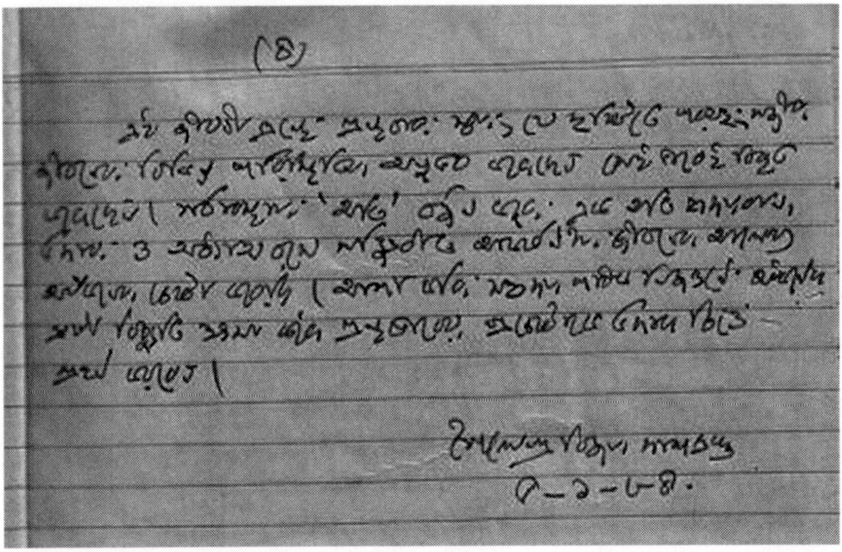

YEAR 2006 PREFACE

Sri Sailendra Bejoy Dasgupta had written this very manuscript near the end of his life in the months of October 1983 through January 1984. In those days that great disciple of Sriyukteshvar Giri had perpetually sat on his bed in yoga posture in the little kitchen room there in Barrackpore (across the river and from Serampore) and he very rarely got up.

Each evening after my Kriya sadhana would be completed the Master liked that I should come and sit beside him and for that purpose he had a chair next to his bed which was considered "my chair." Sitting there together we would have our private and quiet talks about Kriya sadhana as the blanket of night slipped over the sky and the kerosene lamp would be lit. As the shadows danced on the walls we would speak of many things and he would quietly tell me the stories of his Gurudev, Swami Sriyukteshvar Giriji Maharaj or stories of Yogiraj Sri Sri Lahiri Baba or deliver his peerless insights on the Kriya Yoga of Lahiri Mahasay. In front of us was a small table on which we would take our meals. Dadu had several things on the table such as an old Bengali anthropology book (which now sits on the table next to me!) and a small bundle of pencils and so on. Also on that table at that time was this very handwritten Bengali manuscript which he was working on. Each evening he would tell me what he had written that day in the manuscript which contained some accounts concerning his brother disciple, the Paramhansa Yogananda Giri. At this time in his life he was busy putting into writing much of his knowledge of historic Kriya Yoga, both concerning the tradition and history as well as those portions of the traditional technical aspect of Kriya which could be spoken of publicly (see chapter 5 of his book "Kriya Yoga"). This he was doing in order to preserve the historic tradition and knowledge of the events. He had spent his whole life surrounded by Kriya and had personally known several of the direct disciples of the Yogiraj Sri Sri Lahiri Mahasay. He had received Kriya in year 1929 from Sriyukteshvar direct and sat at Swami's feet as an eminent and well loved disciple and as stated, the course of his life had brought him in intimate contact with several illustrious disciples of Yogiraj Sri Sri Lahiri Mahasay such as Shastri Mahasay and others and he also enjoyed close friendship with personages engaged in the preserving of Kriya tradition such as his friend Sri Ananda Mohan Lahiri, a grandson of the Yogiraj (who was on the staff at Yoganandaji's Ranchi school).

Dadu had been in a unique position during Yoganandaji's return visit to India in year 1935-36. At that time a Bengali language secretary was needed (Yoganandaji's disciple Richard Wright had acted as the English language secretary). Due to Dadu's keen intelligence (he had been an eminent scholar of the Calcutta University—First Class First in Anthropology) it naturally came about for him to fill that role and during these months he was almost always in the presence of Yoganandaji and the two developed very great love for each other. It was to accurately record the incidents of that time that Dadu set about to write this book in the end months of his life (Dadu left this earth just weeks after completing this manuscript). His perspective is unique, recording the events from the standpoint of being a spiritual brother and observer.

Revered Swami Satyananda Giri Maharaj (eminent disciple of Sriyukteshvar) had written in his book "Yogananda Sanga" the following—

"During the time that Yoganandaji was in India [after returning from America], Sailendra Bejoy was with him practically all day every day and attended to him in many different ways. Swamiji had a great wish that he would take Sailendra Bejoy to America. Even after [Yoganandaji] went back to America, he wrote to me about this many times. But at that time, Sailendra Bejoy did not particularly have much interest in that direction."

I feel it is relevant to include in this Preface a story which Dadu told me in private as he was writing this manuscript in year 1983. At Dadu's wish I had been staying with him in his house. One sunny afternoon Dadu was in the kitchen working on this book and I had just risen from practicing Kriya. It had been our custom to have our tea and biscuits together in the afternoon each day. That particular day Dadu called me to his side in great joy with a smile on his face. He had been remembering the story of his first meeting with his famous brother disciple, Paramhansa Swami Yogananda. Although the two were both direct disciples of the Swami Maharaj (Swami Sriyukteshvar) the two had never met before that particular day in year 1935. The eventful meeting took place September 18 of that year at the train station in Calcutta. Yoganandaji was triumphantly returning home after spending many years in the western lands. A huge crowd had assembled at the train station to greet him and among that crowd was Dadu.

As Yoganandaji's train pulled into the station the car which contained Swamiji stopped right in front of the exact spot where Dadu was standing. As soon as Swamiji stepped out of the car and onto the platform he saw Dadu and looked directly at him and he said—

"Ah! Here is the biographer!"

We owe many thanks to various Kriyavans who triumphed over tremendously difficult obstacles to tend to the work of translating the hand written manuscript from the original Bengali, in which it is written, and putting it carefully and exactly into the English form found in this book and to those who worked so hard on the matter of publishing. Those selfless workers wish to remain anonymous and so their names cannot be mentioned here. But we remain forever grateful.

It was Sri Dasguptaji's intention that this manuscript be published after being completed but in the time following His passing in March 1984 there was not the means among those of us who sat at His feet to immediately go ahead with the project. Now at this time it is possible and the means are here.

Let the Great One's wish be fulfilled.

Salutations,

n.w. "kashi" ("bala gopee") for
Yoga Niketan Team
Winter Solstice Day
Yoga Niketan
Portland, Maine

DEDICATION

Paramhansa Yogananda himself published his autobiography more than a decade before leaving his body. Since then, his presence has spread through the current of his world-encompassing work. In a highly-paced life, with every year filled with significant events, he was guided in a singular direction through it all: India's ancient and beloved yoga-sadhana—his teaching and establishing of that science as well as its propagation. This one-pointed motion of his life was not restrained by the following and adhering to some previously formulated way; instead, it was as if all of the work was resolutely carried out by the power of some unseen Force. Because of this, the lack of exacting precision regarding the recording of many of the actual happenings has become increasingly evident; on the contrary, because of emotionalism, it has been seen that immaculate versions of those accounts have been accepted.

The guru for the disciple, or the worshipped being for the devotee—it is because such persons of reverence are portrayed as gods—avatars [incarnations of God]—that it brings us such fulfillment in our connection with them; but in the spiritual perspective, every single being is a child of the Eternal—be it guru, be it disciple. The difference between them is only in the state of Divine Experience—a difference of Awakening [or—Revelation]. Bhagavan Sri Sri Sai Baba said summarily in one statement, "I am God; you are also God; I know that I am God, but you don't know that you are God." This fundamental understanding of Truth is substantiated in six [primary] ways in Hindu philosophy. In present times, life-portraits and reminiscent accounts have also been written regarding that field. "Dev-manav"—godman*—these are terms which define a being in whom the attributes of "dev" [deity, god] are intermixed with those of "manav" [human]; they are not excluded from each other. Therefore, all of the qualities of a human being certainly must manifest in the "dev-manav" [godman]. Their exceptional feature is that "God-ness" manifests much more through them. For thousands of years, the teachings of the Hindu scriptures—in study, instruction and sadhana [teachings in practice]—have been devoted to showing human beings the means of attaining the Eternity/Immortality of "Dev." From time to time, the appearance of certain God-intoxicated beings verifies the truth of these universal teachings and provides a visible example to the world. Much of the life of Yogananda was also in this way and is one such example.

[*Translator's note: The word "godman" is in English in the original.]

Yogananda played out his "lila" [divine sport] in this world for 59 years, 2 months and 2 days. He spent more than half of this continuously moving life—almost 32 years—in America, during which time he returned to India and stayed for exactly 3 years. This author was in his very close companionship for one year, during the time Yoganandaji had returned to see and travel his Motherland. However, while attending the Brahmacharya Vidyalaya—a school which was founded by Yoganandaji himself—as a resident brahmachari student in 1928, this writer had already come to know something of his glorious life, particularly from Yoganandaji's childhood companion as well as unfaultable and obedient follower—Swami Satyananda. Satyanandaji was the principal of the Brahmacharya Vidyalaya at that time, and one who acted as a guardian and benefactor to this writer, helping him in every area and every way, so that the writer could be ably established in this life. It is because of Satyanandaji's graciousness that this writer was able to have the wondrous and great fortune of having a place at the feet of Yoganandaji's gurudev, Srimat Swami Sriyukteshvar, and this writer is deeply gratified to have had his blessing and affection. Yoganandaji's life was an "open book." Even though this writer was with him regularly for only one year, upon experiencing the touch of his loving heart and the profundity of his spiritual state, it did not take a great deal of time to get to know the whole person. During his stay in India and for some time after returning to America, Yoganandaji proposed many times that this writer take a vow of sannyas and go with him to America. Although deeply stirred, this writer did not have the good fortune of taking up that priceless proposition at that time. Refusing to accept this, Yoganandaji said, "Now I'm courting you. Later, even if you grind your head you won't get this opportunity." Even the efforts of some opportunistic people attempting to spread slander about this writer in their correspondence with Yoganandaji did not end Swamiji's efforts to take the writer to America. Although Satyanandaji wrote many entreating letters to this writer to clarify the situation with Yoganandaji, this writer himself did not agree to write to Yoganandaji and let him know the truth about what was being said about him [the writer]. Yoganandaji would not settle for this and had said, "I'll return to India and uncover the truth about everything myself. There's no need to write letters." How could

Yoganandaji have been wrong about the man for whom he had had such great affection? The destroyer of vanity—God—annihilates everyone's vain pride. So, shattering this writer's vanity like lightning striking with no clouds in sight, this extraordinary "manav santan" [son of humanity] suddenly left this Earth in 1952. The possibility of talking openly was forever erased; one's pain was destined to remain within forever.

The author of this book gathered most of the material for this book directly from his personal talks with Swami Yoganandaji himself, as well as from personal talks with Yoganandaji's childhood companion Satyanandaji and Swamiji's relatives, friends and students. Some material was collected from "Inner Culture," a journal published by the primary spiritual organization founded by Swamiji in America. But most importantly, this writer was made aware of many hitherto unknown things via three particularly essential ways. First: this writer was blessed with Yoganandaji's affection and trust. Second: this writer was directly initiated by Swamiji's guru Sriyukteshvarji and he was regularly in Sriyukteshvarji's physical company. During this time, this writer was privileged to hear his Gurudev speak descriptively about Yoganandaji carrying out his duties when he was still living in India, as well as Sriyukteshvarji's own feelings at the time and the Divine Grace around such activities. And third: this writer was the exceptional recipient of Swami Satyanandaji's great affection and trust. At an incalculably precious moment in a time when the secret methods of Kriya Yoga sadhana were being spread in India and subsequently in the world, the goddess of fate placed upon this writer this undertaking. Whether the writing of this life-portrait properly carried out this unforeseen service can only be judged by fellow spiritual practitioners and the readers. This book has no intention of spreading any defamation or debating any useless matters.

In English, Bengali and Hindi, this writer's book on Kriya Yoga* covered the endeavors of three extraordinary beings regarding the spreading of Kriya Yoga—Yogiraj Sri Sri Shyama Charan Lahiri, Srimat Swami Sriyukteshvarji and Paramhansa Swami Yogananda. Recently, this writer completed his English work "Ten Eminent Disciples of Banares" (Yogiraj and His Eminent Disciples).** In this book, Yogiraj and Swami Sriyukteshvarji's lives were expounded upon in detail. The life of Yoganandaji could not be included in that book simply because Yoganandaji was not a direct disciple—"shishya"— of Yogiraj; he was Yogiraj's "prashishya"—a disciple of Yogiraj's disciple [Sriyukteshvarji]. For this reason, it was felt that a separate biography of Yoganandaji was necessary. This Bengali version of the book has come to be because the writer felt it easiest to write about the memories of being with

Yoganandaji in Bengali, even though many friends, devotees and interested persons have asked for this biography to be written in English as well.

[*Editor's note: Please see the book "Kriya Yoga" by Sailendra Bejoy Dasgupta at www.yoganiketan.net.]

[**Editor's note: yet to be presented]

The author of this biographical work has simply put to paper the different life-situations with Paramhansaji just as the writer experienced and felt them. Although leaving aside the "extreme and incredible" in every case, this writer has tried to paint the life-portrait of an extremely and incredibly magnanimous, noble, spiritually luminous and magnetic being. It is hoped that the kind readers will forgive any mistakes and discrepancies unknown to the writer and will receive the writer's endeavor with an open heart and mind.

Paramhansa Swami Yogananda Giriji Maharaj

CHAPTER 1
Birth and Preparatory Days

"Man is led not by head but by heart"—this maxim is clearly exemplified and evident in every area of Paramhansa Swami Yogananda's life and his world-wide work. It is proper here to mention a laudatory statement regarding Yoganandaji made by a progressively minded Parsi lady of very high distinction from Bombay. Srimati Firoza Taliyar Khan* has traveled widely, including many places in India, Europe and the United States. She visited and met with Yoganandaji several times at his primary spiritual institution's headquarters at Mount Washington in Los Angeles, and she came to know about every area of Yoganandaji's work. Although she leads the life of a very modern woman, Ms. Firoza Khan is exceptionally knowledgeable about Indian culture and has been in the company of many Godlike saints and sages. She was an ardent devotee and supporter of Bhagavan Ramana Maharshi of Tiruvannamalai. She often resided in a small cottage that she procured near the Maharshi's ashram, and was regularly in his presence. Sometime during the 1930's, this noble and distinguished woman visited the Yogoda Satsanga Ashram in Ranchi for a few days. One day during that time she said to this writer, "I've seen many Godlike saints and spent time in their company as well, and Yogananda is truly great, because he knows how to love." Those who were close to him and who were blessed to be touched by his loving heart are well aware of the truth of this statement. This magnanimity of heart was at the root and center of all of the accomplishments of Yoganandaji's life.

[*Editor's note: Saintly Srimati Firoza Taliyar Khan, or "Mother Thalaiyar Khan," had great love for the devotees of God and she used to visit them all, from Anandamoyee Ma to Yogananda Paramhansa. In her Autobiography entitled "Arunachala Ramana," she has recounted how she received darshan of one of the forms of Divine Mother (Tulija-Bhavani) at the age of eight. From her childhood she received loving guidance in meditation from a divine form. She came to Bhagavan Ramana Maharshi and stayed in Arunachalam. As a lofty spiritual devotee, she faced severe trials of life to stay in the path.]

1

The biographer has a very difficult responsibility. Himself being the recipient of the love and respect of such a soul, the writer is bound and compelled to a perspective directed by his greatest influence. One is pulled to portray everything in a brilliant life only from that side. Because of this, it is not a simple task to draw an impersonal and complete picture of the person. In 1935 Yoganandaji had returned to India and this writer went to visit him at Swamiji's residence. Upon seeing the writer, Swamiji turned to his American personal secretary Charles Richard Wright and said, "Look, look! Doesn't he look just like Mahadev Desai?" After arriving in Bombay from America, Swamiji had taken a detour from his train journey to Calcutta and had gone to Wardha to see Mahatma Gandhi at Gandhiji's ashram. There Swamiji had met Mahatmaji's personal secretary, biographer and publisher of the "Navajivan" journal—Mahadev Desai. There must have been some similarity in the appearances of Mahadev Desai and this writer, hence that remark. Perhaps it was because in those days this writer used to dress in plain cotton dhoti and kurta when attending to his full-time responsibilities with Yoganandaji. Swamiji used to introduce this writer as "My Indian personal secretary." Sometimes as soon as he would see the writer, he would speak out, "Here comes the biographer." Of course, he addressed the writer in this way only out of love and affection. The writer could not even imagine at that time that someday long afterwards—almost a half-century later—he would be endeavoring to write the biography of Swamiji himself. Perhaps this is how the spontaneous impressions in the minds of realized beings and prophecies that spring forth from their saintly mouths become fulfilled.

Birth and Childhood

In the final decade of the 19th century, on January 5, 1896 a child was born to a Bengali couple residing in the town of Gorakhpur in what is now known as the province of Uttar Pradesh. Named Mukunda Lal, later in life this child would be known as Swami Yogananda and eventually as Paramhansa Swami Yogananda. Father Bhagabati Charan Ghosh kept his household in Icchapur in the 24 Pargana District of Bengal. But because of being in an administrative position in governmental service, he often had to travel to Uttar Pradesh, Punjab and other places outside of Bengal for his work. Bhagabati Charan was respected as a dedicated, serious-minded, highly-skilled and proficient administrator. Gyanprabha Devi was a devout wife, pious and religiously observant, and the epitome of a loving and affectionate mother. Exceedingly beautiful, she was the possessor of a pair of indescribably striking eyes—eyes in which Mukunda Lal felt the Mother of the Universe. All of Mukunda Lal's brothers and sisters were born with their mother's stunning eyes. A few years before Mukunda Lal's birth, Bhagabati Charan and his wife were initiated into the practice of Kriya Yoga by Kashi Baba Yogiraj Sri Sri Shyama Charan Lahiri. It was as if a dictum of the Bhagavad Gita had become exemplified: the result of Mukunda Lal's beneficent efforts in his previous life had awarded him a priceless birth in a household of yogis.

Bhagabati Charan and Gyanprabha Devi had eight children—four boys and four girls. Mukunda Lal was the fourth. Brother Ananta Lal was the eldest; after him was eldest sister Roma Devi and middle sister Uma Devi. Mukunda Lal and Roma Devi were very close. The third daughter was Surjabati Devi and the youngest of the girls was Nalini Devi who was very dear to Mukunda Lal. Brother Sananda Lal was the seventh child, and the youngest of all of the children was brother Bishnu Charan. Bhagabati Charan spoke sparingly and was of a somber nature, and his children looked up to him with deference and respect. Mother Gyanprabha was the opposite; full of expressive affection, she was the embodiment of compassion and extremely religious. The children were primarily brought up in their mother's influence. For Mukunda Lal his mother was life itself. Gyanprabha Devi would often be taken aback and concerned by signs of her dear son's uncommonly spiritual nature and extraordinary supernatural abilities, even as a child. When she took Mukunda Lal in his infancy to Sri Guru Yogiraj Shyama Charan for His blessings, the Great Yogi held the child in His lap and said, "I see that this boy will be an engine in the future." Perhaps this prophetic statement of blessing was an indication of the future when Yoganandaji would become the spiritual guru and helmsman of life for innumerable people.

The Late Bhagabati Charan Ghosh Mahasaya
Paramhansa Swami Yogananda Giri Maharaj's Father

Loss of Mother and Signs of the Sannyas Way of Life to Come

Mukunda Lal lost his mother at a very early age—in 1904, when he was only eleven years old. Bishnu Charan was still an infant, unable yet to crawl. And as fate would have it, Mukunda Lal could not be present at the side of his loving mother at the time of her departure. She had come to Calcutta to make arrangements for the upcoming marriage of her eldest son Ananta Lal, and her husband and son Mukunda Lal were staying in a house in the town of Berili [Birla] for the time being. But before she could begin to attend to the arrangements, she suddenly fell ill. Mukunda Lal dreamt at night that his beloved mother was in a terrible state in Calcutta; there was no hope of her staying alive. Right from his bed, he screamed out to his father that his mother would not live. His father tried to calm him down by saying that events in dreams do not become true and such things like this, and somehow they passed the night. But Bhagabati Charan received a telegram early that very morning saying that his wife was gravely afflicted and bedridden. Immediately, father and son made haste and took the very next train to Calcutta. But Mukunda Lal did not get to see her one last time. By the time of their arrival, she was gone—leaving all. There was a strange incident that had happened previously that shadowed over this rush to make arrangements for Ananta Lal's wedding. Some days before, Bhagabati

Charan was with his family in Lahore [in what is now known as Pakistan]. One day, in the middle of the day when Bhagabati Charan was away at work, an elderly sannyasi knocked on the door of the Ghosh residence. Just as Gyanprabha Devi opened the door, the holy man walked in and said that he was directed by a great Himalayan saint to come there. He handed an amulet to Gyanprabha Devi and said that that amulet should be given to Mukunda Lal one year after her death. The sannyasi also said that Gyanprabha Devi's lifespan had come to its end and that the illness that would befall her in the coming days would be the cause of her death. He continued and told her that Mukunda Lal would not lead a householder's life; he would become a sannyasi and renounce worldly life, and as soon as he found his Sadguru, the sacred amulet would go away by itself. Because of her impending demise, Gyanprabha Devi became deeply concerned about who would take over the household duties of the family—hence the haste to make arrangements for her eldest son's marriage. She wrote down the words spoken by the sannyasi on a small piece of paper, very carefully placed the paper and the amulet in a small closed container and kept it constantly with her. In Calcutta, when she saw that her time of death was approaching, she called Ananta Lal by her side and told him to keep this container under great care, to never open it himself, and give it directly to Mukunda one year after her death.

Attraction to the Himalayas

After the loss of his mother, Mukunda Lal felt as if his world was one great void. His only sanctuary was his affectionate mother's tenderness and her incredibly beautiful eyes—the only place of serenity and security. Losing that ever-loving one, his heart no longer wanted to stay home. His spirit constantly craved to escape life in the world, and it was as if the Himalayas were calling him to come. His mother had taught him to keep secret within his heart his longing to lay his head at the Feet of the Universal Mother, and now it seemed to him that he would find that same Universal Mother in the mountains of the Himalayas. This feeling was constantly awake in him and made him restless and wanting to leave. He even tried to run away from home to the Himalayas and got as far as Nainital, but he was not able to escape his eldest brother Ananta Lal's alertness and had to return home from there. Still, he always felt the calling of the Himalayas within him.

In the Company of Saints at an Early Age

Fourteen months after their mother's death, Ananta Lal presented Mukunda Lal with the small container he had received from Gyanprabha Devi. Upon opening the box containing the amulet and reading the letter accompanying it, Mukunda was overcome. The nectarous memories of his virtuous and compassionate mother flooded his eyes with loving tears, and having received direction at the same time from an unknown Great Power Who was invisibly governing his destiny of spirituality, his heart overflowed with joy.

Ananta Lal and father Bhagabati Charan had always been aware of Mukunda Lal's intense longing for the spiritual way of life, and they also noticed aloofness towards worldly life rise in him after his mother's death. Fearing that he may again try to run away from home, they tried to keep an eye on him at all times. Regardless of this, when from time to time he would find out about some sages and saints coming nearby, Mukunda Lal would sneak away from his family and secretly go and visit them. In order to satisfy Mukunda Lal's desire to go around and see spiritual persons, Bhagabati Charan let him travel to many places. One of these times, he went to Benares [Varanasi]. Mukunda Lal was twelve years old. Bhagabati Charan had two friends in Benares, Kedar Babu and Swami Pranabananda Giri. Mukunda Lal stayed at Kedar Babu's house. One day, Kedar Babu went to bathe in the Ganges and Mukunda Lal was visiting Swami Pranabanandaji's hermitage. Mukunda Lal sat in front of a meditating Pranabanandaji, seated in yogic posture and absorbed in Divine Ecstasy. Just a short while afterwards, Mukunda Lal was surprised to see that Kedar Babu had left the Ganges and was coming in their direction. As soon as Kedar Babu came near, Mukunda Lal asked how he came here so quickly, thinking that Kedar Babu would still be by the riverside. Kedar Babu pointed to Pranabanandaji and answered that it was Swamiji himself who had come to the banks of the Ganges and had asked him to come. Mukunda Lal was stupefied. Swamiji was always in front of him, absorbed in meditation! When could he have gone to the banks? And so, right at that early age, Mukunda Lal realized that this type of extraordinary act could only be performed by a great yogi. In later life as Swami Yogananda, he would speak descriptively about this act by the miraculous power of Pranabanandaji in many gatherings and talks around the world.*

*[English Editor's note: We were told the following rare stories about Swami Pranabanandaji by our friend who is a direct disciple of Pranabanandaji's

eminent disciple, the late Sri Jnanendra Mukhopadyay. Our friend had heard these stories direct from the mouth of the late Sri Jnanendra:

Before Swami Pranabananda left this world he told his followers that after his death they should put his body inside a trunk (box) and keep it immersed in the holy Ganges water for one night and next morning they should lift the trunk and do the required formalities. So accordingly the disciples put his body inside a trunk after death & locked it and tied the trunk with chain so that it would not float away and immersed it in Ganges water and waited throughout the night on the bank of the Ganges. The next morning they lifted out the trunk and found it was still locked but yet was empty! His body was not found! His body had vanished.

Swami Pranabananda had a Siddhi (power) of producing Khichri (a mixture of rice & pulse) as much as he wanted to. He used to cover a container with cloth then removing only half portion of the cloth he used to take out ready made Khichri. When the half portion of khichri was finished he used to cover the empty part of the container with cloth & open the other half portion which was found to be filled with khichri. In this way alternatively the khichri was produced automatically & endlessly. That is why a lot of beggars and sadhus used to take free meals there in Varanasi, Pranabashram. So gradually Swamiji felt disturbed due to a huge crowd of people. He wanted to give it up. Then one day a greedy brahmin asked him to give him this siddhi. He told him to come to the Ganga early in the morning & he will give him the siddhi & if he fails he will give it to the Ganges. Next morning the brahmin did not come so Pranabanandaji gave this siddhi to Ganges and was happy to get rid of the huge crowd.]

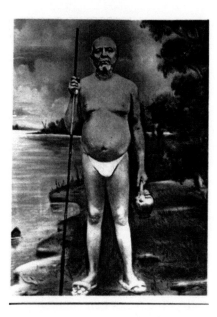

Srimat Swami Pranabananda
(Lofty disciple of Lahiri Mahasaya)

Living in Calcutta

In 1906, Bhagabati Charan permanently transferred to Calcutta. Mukunda Lal was thirteen years old at that time. His family enrolled him in Calcutta's prestigious Hindu School. Although quite thin in physical stature in those days, morally and mentally he was very strong. If he saw any wrongdoing, he would dive into the conflict fearlessly, regardless of whether the opponent was more powerful. There was a particularly tough bully among his classmates; all of the others were terrorized by this "macho" boy. One day, Mukunda Lal protested some improper incident caused by this bully and, following a heated argument, challenged the "macho" boy to a duel of sorts. After an intense fight, Mukunda Lal defeated this bully. His schoolmates were astounded by Mukunda Lal's courage and ability to defend himself, and after that singular incident, he was respected and loved by all of his peers.

Beginnings of Becoming a Spiritual Teacher

Even while he was studying at the Hindu School, whenever he would receive news of any sages and saints in the vicinity, he would immediately hide away from his eldest brother's watchful eyes and escape to go and see them and be in their company. At about this time, Bhagabati Charan bought a house at No. 4 Garpar Road and became a permanent resident of Calcutta. Exactly opposite this house, on the south side of the street, was the Calcutta Deaf and Dumb School. The late Mohini Mohan Majumdar, the eminent founder—and professor—of this university, lived in the residence quarters of the school as the superintendent of the dormitory. His son Manomohan Majumdar was often with him. Although Manomohan was five or six years younger than Mukunda Lal, a deep friendship formed between them within a very short time. Manomohan was captivated and taken by Mukunda Lal's natural spiritual awareness, his deep reverence for saints and sages and resolute aspiration to live the spiritual life. Unbeknownst to himself, Manomohan had not only become Mukunda Lal's friend but also his disciple and follower.* Mukunda Lal did not wait long to teach everything about meditation and spiritual practice he had learned from his loving mother and his eldest sister Roma Devi to his young friend-disciple. Going together to see saints and sages, visiting Belur Math, Dakshineshwar Temple and such holy places, meditating together, sometimes sitting together in meditative absorption in some place of solitude away from the city at night—all such things became a regular part of their lives. It was only natural that Mukunda Lal took the position of guru. And this was somewhat true at the Hindu School as well. Although most of his classmates may not have been so spiritual-minded, many of the youths of good character were attracted to Mukunda Lal and were fascinated by his virtues. One among them who became particularly devoted to Mukunda Lal was Amar Mitra of the Mitra family from Kumartoli. Even in his neighborhood in Garpar, quite a few friends and relatives held Mukunda Lal in very high regard. Their reason for associating with Mukunda Lal was primarily to discuss religious and spiritual things.

[*Publisher's note: Manomohan Majumdar [Swami Satyananda Giri] is referred to as Yoganandaji's disciple" in only an informal sense. This is an expression of the deep respect and love Satyanandaji held for his elder brother Yoganandaji. Satyanandaji and Yoganandaji had not yet met their formal Guru in Kriya Yoga who was none other than Swami Sriyukteshvar Giri. As Satyanandaji writes in Yogananda Sanga:

"It is needless to say that because this servant [Satyanandaji] has had the company of Swami Sriyukteshvar Giri Maharaj, it is he [Sriyukteshvarji] who holds the place as 'Guru Maharaj' for this servant." (Swami Satyananda Giri from Yogananda Sanga Chapter 1)]

Swami Satyananda Giriji Maharaj
Eminent and faithful disciple of Swami Sriyukteshvar
and childhood friend of Yogananda

But the longing to go to the Himalayas was ever awake in Mukunda Lal's heart. Never had the desire subsided for having the darshan [blessed sightings] of yogis and realized beings, and finding his life-helmsman Sadguru. He began to confer with his closest friends about finding a way to escape to the Himalayas.

Escaping for the Himalayas

One day, three young friends—Mukunda Lal, Amar Mitra and Jotin Ghosh—planned to run away to Hardwar [Haridvar—in the foothills of the Himalayas]. Making up an excuse that they were just going for an outing in the vicinities around Calcutta, they went directly to the Howrah train station instead. Remembering his brother's alert watchfulness, Mukunda Lal even made arrangements to change into different clothes during their journey. Amar Mitra brought a horse-drawn carriage to Garpar, feigning that he and friend Mukunda Lal were just going out and about in Calcutta; they somehow secretly loaded a small-sized bundle onto the carriage as they were leaving. Jotin Ghosh then joined them. So that brother Ananta Lal would not easily catch on to where they were headed, they first bought tickets to Burdwan [Bardhaman—in Bengal] at the Howrah station. The plan was that they would get off at Burdwan and buy another set of tickets for Hardwar and head that way in the morning. After they reached the station in Burdwan, Jotin suddenly ran away as they were preparing to get tickets to Hardwar. After waiting for quite a while, the two of them realized that Jotin was not coming back and that he had probably gone back to Calcutta. However, Amar and Mukunda Lal were steadfast in pursuing their goal; they were going to go to Hardwar, no matter what. Purchasing upper class train tickets, the two of them headed towards Hardwar. When Yoganandaji came back to India from America, Jotin-da* came to see his relative, leader and friend from their adolescent years. After sharing heartfelt greetings and joyful embraces, at one point, Jotin-da stretched out on Swamiji's bed and Swamiji humorously recounted the story of that secret adventure. As Swamiji descriptively spoke about Jotin-da's "act of fear" and running back home, Jotin-da also laughed and joined in on this jocularity. Swamiji was yelping out in laughter and trying to "pull Jotin-da's leg." That was a wonderful scene to behold.

[*Translator's note: The Bengali suffix "da"—literally meaning "elder brother"—is often used to denote a sign of casual respect and is not restricted to family members only. "Babu" and "Mahasaya" are the Bengali adjuncts for addressing someone more formally.]

Bhagabati Charan and Ananta Lal became deeply worried as Mukunda had not returned home. Everyone was full of anxiety at Amar Mitra's house as well. News of this was spread out; the police were also informed. Ananta Lal did not take long to figure out that they may be traveling to Hardwar. Information about them were given to the police networks covering India and the police were now allowed to arrest them and bring them back. Mukunda and Amar had already assumed that this type of thing may happen and they were prepared to fool the police as well. They had taken Western clothes with them in their bundle and had changed into them during the journey. When the train reached the Mogulsarai Junction, a police officer spotted them and began to ask questions. The fearless Amar Mitra convinced the officer that one of them was named "Thomas" and the other "Thompson". Not only was the officer satisfied with this answer, he actually apologized to the young gentlemen for disturbing them and asked for their forgiveness. But this tactic did not work in Hardwar. As they disembarked at the station, they were both immediately taken by the waiting police to the station master's office. Within two days, Ananta Lal and Amar Mitra's elder brother arrived, ready to take their brothers back home. Amar agreed to return without much hesitation but Mukunda protested heavily. In the end, both had to go back to Calcutta with their elder brothers. Father Bhagabati Charan's agonizing anxiety was finally quelled. And this time, Bhagabati Charan gave strict orders to Mukunda Lal that he must promise not to leave home until he at least passed his Entrance Exams. However, the habit of being with sages and running to see sadhus and yogis as soon as he would hear of their proximity never stopped—still eluding Ananta Lal's watchful eyes.

At this time, there were two places to which Mukunda Lal went—almost as a regular discipline: Belur Math with his companions and friends, and No. 50 Amherst Street, the residence of "Master Mahasaya" Sri Mahendra Nath Gupta, also known as Sri "M"—the author of the Gospel of Sri Ramakrishna. Swami Prajnananda—or "Rakhal Maharaj"—who was the president of the Sri Ramakrishna Mission, loved Mukunda Lal very much. Whenever Mukunda Lal would go to the Belur Math, Swamiji would call him over and affectionately say, "Mukunda is 'our' boy." To go and see Sri "M" in the afternoon was more or less a daily routine. First, Sri "M"s residence was not very far from Garpar Road, but besides that, there was something else that drew Mukunda to that place. His beloved mother had drawn her last breath in an apartment they were renting in that very building. Mukunda Lal experienced several spiritually revelatory experiences with Sri "M" and because of this he revered Sri "M" like his guru. He had even beseeched Sri "M" to please accept him as a disciple. Once he had made the same request to Rakhal Maharaj as well. But both of them gave Mukunda Lal the same answer, "I am not your guru. Your guru is coming. You will have him very soon."

A little while after settling permanently in Calcutta, Bhagabati Charan retired from governmental service. During the term of his employment, word had spread to eminent trading companies and railway services about his management and accounting skills, and the executives of these firms held him in very high regard. It was heard that he had masterfully and swiftly resolved a heavy financial burden that had been outstanding for many years in the Eastern Bengal Railway Company. In those days, all of the rail companies in India were run by British firms. After thirty years of straight service in governmental work, when Bhagabati Charan began to receive his pension upon reaching the age of fifty and retired from that work, the Bengal Nagpur Railway immediately enlisted his services in a high and powerful position in their company. He became the P.A. (personal assistant) of the Company Agent. The "Agent" of a British company was the executive in charge of every facet of the entire enterprise, and being his P.A. meant receiving exceptional financial remuneration as well as power. It was actually the P.A. that carried out the daily responsibilities of the Agent. In those days, it was virtually unthinkable for an Indian to reach such a position at a British company; it is not difficult to surmise the level of respect this drew from society. Bhagabati Charan held this position for many years.

Being in the Company of Acharya Shastri Mahasaya

At the time of the "Himalayan escape," Mukunda Lal's home tutor was a respectable man of erudition named Rakhal Kabiraj. Although he was not a spiritual practitioner [sadhak], he often engaged the spiritually inclined Mukunda Lal in discussions about many aspects of philosophy and spiritual teachings. After Mukunda Lal's flight towards the mountains, Ananta Lal firmly concluded that it was this elderly Sri Kabiraj Mahasaya who was the cause of this; talking about nothing but spiritual and philosophical things all the time corrupted his brother's mind. It was decided that he should no longer be kept as home tutor. He was replaced by an ordinary-looking, soft-spoken teacher from the Metropolitan High School named Sri Ashutosh Shastri. It was not possible to guess from this man's demeanor that he was a scholar of the highest level. Furthermore, Ananta Lal did not have the slightest inkling of Shastri Mahasaya's immensely advanced stage of spirituality. He could not imagine in any way at the depths of water in which this "fish" swam, and ironically it was in the waters that Ananta Lal feared in the first place. How could he have known that in trying to rescue him from spirituality that he would actually be handing his spiritually mad brother over to a "spiritual bandit"?! By the time Ananta Lal realized that not only did his father Bhagabati Charan and this new tutor know each other, but that they were also "guru-brothers" [disciples of the same guru], it was too late and Shastri Mahasaya's position was now beyond Ananta Lal's power. This new teacher Ashutosh Shastri Mahasaya was not just a disciple of Yogiraj Shayama Charan Lahiri Mahasaya; he was an eminently advanced Kriya Yogi and yoga-guru. Thus, what happens when like minds meet began to happen. In the name of academic studies, the teaching of Kriya Yoga and its practice went on behind closed doors. And the study and analysis of the meanings of the Gita and other such essential scriptures also went on as an adjunct. Mukunda Lal was extremely happy that together they were finally able to evade his brother's sentry-like watch.

It is at this time that Mukunda Lal's training in spiritual work began. The association with Manomohan Majumdar has already been mentioned. Now, joining him were schoolmate Upendra Nath Mitra from Garpar, Tulsi Narayan Basu (the son of the principal of the Calcutta Art School, Sri Hari

Narayan Basu) and Jitendra Lal Majumdar who was studying at the Herr School and was of the same age as Mukunda Lal. There was a young admirer-friend of Tulsi Narayan named Prakash Chandra Das, who was much younger than Tulsi Narayan. Prakash Chandra's family was deeply involved with the newly founded Brahmo Samaj; he was very intelligent and sharp in mind. He also came with Tulsi Narayan and joined this congregation from time to time. Jitendra Nath's father was an eminent businessman in the paper industry in Calcutta; he was known to have only traveled in trams and buses until his personal net worth had accumulated to at least 100,000 rupees. It was only after he attained this goal that he purchased a car. Of course "car" in those days meant horse-drawn carriages—Landau carriages; the practice of driving automobiles had not become that prevalent yet. He also had a palatial mansion built on Rani Swarnamayi Road. Eldest son Upendra Lal Majumdar was the heir to his father's business. Jitendra Lal, fair in complexion, was very attractive physically and in behavior as well. Mukunda Lal's brothers and sisters were all very drawn to fair-skinned boys and girls. Although every one of them had inherited their mother's wondrously beautiful eyes, all of them were basically dark in complexion. Perhaps one reason for Mukunda Lal's exceptional love for Jitendra Lal was because of the color of his skin. It was at Upendra Nath Mitra's house that Mukunda Lal began his regular gatherings of spiritual discussions. Of course, Manomohan was there, following like a shadow, and the above-mentioned new friends also began to join in. Among them, Tulsi Narayan was particularly drawn to Belur Math. As the number of friends continued to grow, the place of congregation was moved to a one-storey house adjoining Tulsi Narayan's family home.

Loved and Blessed by Sri "M"

It has been previously mentioned that Mukunda Lal spent time with Master Mahasaya Mahendra Nath Gupta every day. It has also been stated that Mukunda Lal had had certain supernatural experiences with him. A couple of such incidents are being put to paper here, as heard by this writer directly from Yoganandaji's own mouth. One day, sometime around midday, Mukunda went to Master Mahasaya's residence; possibly it was a holiday. Master Mahasaya was not in his room. Mukunda looked out and saw that he was standing outside on the roof,* looking up at the sky and laughing heartily and seemingly talking to someone. Mukunda quickly ran to him and with great curiosity asked, "Master Mahasaya! Who are you talking to?" Without returning any answer whatsoever, Master Mahasaya continued to look up at the sky and laugh and laugh. Mukunda's curiosity was fueled even more, and with a beseeching tone of voice, he asked again, "Who are you talking to? Won't you please tell me? Please, won't you tell me?" Master Mahasaya had had great affection for this dear child. Eventually, he turned to Mukunda and, completely astonishing him, said, "With Mother." Mukunda's excitement intensified even more: "I also want to see Mother! And talk to Her!" As Mukunda continued to beg and demand for this to happen, Master Mahasaya finally said, "It will happen later." With uncontrollable eagerness Mukunda Lal asked, "When will it happen?" The answer was again, "Later." From this point on, every single day, Mukunda would ask Master Mahasaya, "Won't you please tell me, when it will happen?" And he had to hear the same answer every day, "Later."

[*Translator's note: Rooftops in India are, in most cases, habitable and with a protective wall surrounding the edges of the roof.]

In the meantime, dodging his brother's watch, Mukunda would sit for meditation every day at dusk in their house's storage room. One day, his mind became very absorbed as he was meditating, and a short while after that he had a vision of the Goddess Kali. His heart danced with joy. But he kept this experience completely to himself. Next afternoon, as was his daily ritual to do so, he went to see Master Mahasaya. And immediately upon seeing him, Mukunda again asked in that pleading tone of voice, "Every day you say 'it will happen later, it will happen later, it will happen later.' But why don't you tell me when it will happen?" Master Mahasaya did not answer back. Mukunda again said insistently, "Is this how sadhus are? You give your word and you don't keep it! All you say is 'it will happen later!'" Then Master Mahasaya grinned and said, "Are you being mischievous or what?" Mukunda said, "What mischief? You gave your word that you will show me Mother. Where have you kept your word?" Master Mahasaya looked directly into his eyes and spoke out, "Why—oh about eight o'clock or so last night? In the storage room?" As soon as Mukunda Lal heard this, he fell and hugged Master Mahasaya's feet. Master Mahasaya lifted him up in loving embrace.

First Uses of Mental Power

There was an incident that Mukunda Lal caused which was associated with his secretly meditating every day in the storage room. From his very birth, he was the possessor of an extraordinary ability. Sometimes certain statements would spring forth from him that would unfailingly come true. During childhood when his family was living in Northwest India, a boil appeared on his sister Uma Devi's foot one day. As she was nursing it by applying balm on it, Mukunda Lal showed up from somewhere and started to massage the same balm on his own hand. Uma Devi yelled at him, to which Mukunda Lal said, "Look sister. Tomorrow this boil you have will grow twice its size and a boil will appear on my hand here." The regular bickering between these two close siblings was well known in the family. But the next day, Uma Devi's boil really did grow twice its size, causing her pain as well, and a boil appeared on Mukunda's hand. Mother Gyanprabha Devi was well aware of these "qualities" of her son. She tried to reason with Mukunda that one should not cause other people this kind of pain. There was a also similar incident of will power associated with his meditating in the storage room. This type of power was demonstrated by him many times in later life; this writer himself has directly witnessed it. Only the Oriya* cook of the house knew about his secret meditation sittings in the storage space. One day, the cook more or less jokingly said, "See here 'middle sir'. I will tell 'big sir' about your hiding around and meditating in the storage room." "Big sir" was Ananta Lal. It was wholly disagreeable to Mukunda Lal that his daily spiritual duty would come to an end; he became very angry upon hearing this type of threat. But controlling himself, he simply said, "Look. If I wish, your hand will be stuck to the wall." The cook challenged him, "Let's see how you can do that!" Mukunda Lal took the cook's left palm and put it up against the wall, kept it extended from his body, and counted "1,2,3,4,5,6" and immediately, the cook's hand became locked to the wall. He could not pull himself off no matter how much he tried. He begged, "Sir, please release my hand!" Mukunda said, "Stand here just like this. This is your punishment." And then he went out to play with his mates and forgot about the whole thing. Panchakoti [the cook] was in a sense "handcuffed" to the wall. Gradually, evening came. The work in the kitchen area was completely at a standstill. People in the household also started to wonder where their cook was; finally they were astounded to find him standing there in that condition. The cook tearfully said that it was "middle sir" who had put him in this predicament. The news went to Bhagabati Charan. Upon coming there and seeing this situation, he cried out, "Where is that dastardly son of mine?" Right at that time, Mukunda Lal returned home. Suddenly he remembered what he had left behind. He ran to the cook, touched his hand and the hand was free. The cook fell to Mukunda Lal's feet, begged forgiveness and said that he would never again try to do anything against him. Mukunda replied in a reproaching tone, "You won't ever do this again, right?" The cook pulled his ears in a gesture of being ashamed and said that he would never do it again. The members of the household were stupefied by this whole happening, and they all breathed a collective sigh of relief after it was over. In 1935, when Yoganandaji had returned from America he recounted this story to us one day, and no one could help laughing at his descriptive telling of it, imitating the cook and his condition.

[*Translator's note: "Oriya"—person from the province of Orissa.]

The days passed on like this, but at the same time, the Entrance Exams were fast approaching. Mukunda Lal's schoolmates were working diligently at preparing for the tests. But he was "treading in deep waters." Where's the time to study when you're consumed with spiritual practice and spending time with saints and sages? He would have been very happy to not have to sit for the exams at all, but then again, he had promised his father that he would forsake his desire to leave home until he at least took the exams. So, there was no way out. He had to sit for the tests. Mukunda Lal thought about things for a while and decided that he would take the help of a fellow schoolmate who lived in their very neighborhood—a very good student. As soon as he requested this schoolmate to help him, the boy immediately agreed and happily promised to help in any way possible. Mukunda went to his house every day with all of his schoolbooks and such. Laboring incessantly, he felt at one point that he had made some sort of progress in preparing for the tests. In due time, the exams were held. When the results were announced, it was seen that somehow, by some kind of grace, Mukunda Lal actually passed the Entrance Exams. Now the waves of renunciation again began to sway his entire being. But because of his schoolmates and his father's insistence, he enrolled in the Metropolitan College. But can one who is a "wild bird" at heart ever be happy in a cage? His spirit cried out within, "Run! Run!" And right at this time, he was blessed with yet another wondrous supernatural experience with Master Mahasaya.

Revelation of the Divine through Sri "M"

As was his regular routine, Mukunda went to Master Mahasaya's residence one afternoon. On this day Master Mahasaya was getting ready to go out. After he got dressed he said to Mukunda Lal, "Come. Let's go to the cinema." Mukunda immediately agreed. It wasn't that the cinema was of much interest; he simply wanted to spend time with Master Mahasaya. They went out to the street and took a horse-drawn taxi. The cab had two long seats that faced each other and it was quite comfortable to travel in these carriages. Master Mahasaya and Mukunda Lal sat side by side in the seat facing the front. On the way Master Mahasaya spoke about many spiritual things and of course, Mukunda was elated out of his head at this. After going a little distance, an elderly gentleman saw them and shouted out, "O Master

Mahasaya! Where are you going? Stop, stop! I'll join you!" Without any way out of this, they had to stop the carriage; this gentleman got into the cab and sat in the facing seat. He began to speak about many things about regular worldly life. Mukunda Lal became quite irritated inside. They were having a conversation about such nice things and this man came and ruined everything. At that time, the carriage was trotting through Cornwalis Street. Master Mahasaya leaned over to Mukunda's ear and whispered, "You don't like this—hm? You see that lamp post ahead? As soon as we reach there this man will get out of the car." Just as the carriage reached the spot by the lamp post, the man suddenly cried out, "Stop the car! I left something at home! I have to get off!" The carriage was immediately stopped and the gentleman left. Relieved, Mukunda resumed his conversation with Master Mahasaya. When the carriage was passing by the University Senate House, they saw that there was some sort of conference taking place there; many people had gathered. Master Mahasaya had the carriage stopped, took Mukunda by the hand and said, "Come. Let's go and hear what is being said at this meeting." They found two seats next to each other in the hall and began to listen to the lecture that was going on. Mukunda was getting completely annoyed at having to listen to the talk, and right at this time Master Mahasaya said, "You don't like this, hm? In just a little while all the lights will go out and we'll sneak out of here." Just a few moments later, suddenly the lights all went out, and the hall was filled with the yelling and screaming of the audience. Master Mahasaya grabbed Mukunda's hand and said, "Ok, this is our chance. Come on, let's get out of here." As soon as they both got out of the hall, they saw that all of the lights had come back on inside. They went down the stairs and on to the sidewalk. After walking a little distance to the place where the Herr statue stood, Master Mahasaya stopped in front of the statue and said, "So, we didn't get to see the cinema, hm?" Saying this, he touched Mukunda in the forehead and chest. Immediately, Mukunda lost all body-consciousness; it was as if he was floating somewhere in space. He could see everything and on all sides. He could even see inside the trees and the fluids they were drawing from the earth. He did not remember for how long this state lasted. When Master Mahasaya again touched his body, Mukunda Lal finally came back to body-consciousness. Saying, "So now that we've seen the cinema, let's go home," Master Mahasaya began to turn back. Overcome with reverence, love and gratitude, Mukunda fell and embraced Master Mahasaya's feet. Again he asked to be taken as a disciple. The Shakti-endowed sadhak Master Mahasaya answered, "I'm not your guru. He will be coming into your life very soon."

Second Escape from Home and Finding Sadguru

A short while after enrolling in college, Mukunda Lal determined within himself that enough had been done in this area, no more; now it was time to go out to find Sadguru. And he did just that, taking with him his companion and follower-disciple Jitendra Lal Majumdar; he said nothing of this to his father. Mukunda Lal decided that he would first go to Benares, practice sadhana there and search for his guru. So one day, the two friends quietly set forth towards Benares, and Mukunda Lal took the small container with the amulet from the unknown sage that his mother had passed on to him. They had no idea where they would go in Benares, where they would stay— nothing. They wandered around. Fortunately they came upon a chance meeting with Paramhansa Swami Jnanananda, the head sannyasi [monk] of a spiritual center called "Bharat Dharma Mahamandal." Upon seeing these two youths—not yet adults—dressed in garb associated with celibates, Jnanananda Maharaj surmised that they must have run away from home to become sadhus. After questioning them, he found that his supposition was correct, and finding out that they had no place to stay in Benares, he took them in to stay at his ashram. At the ashram, Jnananandaji let them know clearly that the life of a sannyasi is extremely difficult; one has to prepare oneself for that way of life. He proposed that they stay at the ashram for sadhana, devotional service and scriptural study and that he would make them fit for the renunciate way of life. Mukunda took a liking to this mahatma. He was overjoyed at having a separate cottage at the ashram. He began to practice sadhana with his whole being, but he also had to perform other ashramic duties. Others in the ashram berated him for his obsession with sadhana. All the things of daily life he had abandoned to come here for sannyas—he had to do the same tasks, and also lowly tasks that he did not ever have to do at home! And on top of that, Mukunda Lal could not tolerate sentiments of disregard for meditative practices. No. He determined he had to leave this ashram too. One day, Mukunda Lal was sent to the market with a co-worker to purchase some things for the ashram. As they walked along in the streets of Benares, on the opposite side of an intersection of two roads, he saw a tall, majestic sage, with long, flowing hair, coming towards him from the other road. There was a momentary distraction in the bustle of the crowd at the intersection, but as Mukunda looked again, he saw that the saint was looking steadily at him. Immediately upon seeing his gaze, Mukunda began to feel an intense magnetic pull towards the sage. Mukunda continued to walk in the direction he was walking, but as he looked again, the sage was standing there and still looking unwaveringly at him. In a few moments, Mukunda was out of the sage's sight, but it seemed that his feet would no longer move; they did not want to keep going in that direction any more. The image of that sadhu at the intersection seemed to take over his mind and heart and he could not think of anything else. He gave the money for the market to the person accompanying him, turned and moved quickly back towards that intersection. He saw that the sage was still standing in that same spot he had seen him before. Shouting "Gurudev! Gurudev!" Mukunda ran to the saint and fell at his feet. The saint picked him up, embraced him and said, "Thou hast come at last my boy!"* Although not introduced yet in this life, they had known each other since time immemorial—tied together by one string. That mysterious sage was Swami Sriyukteshvar Giri himself, Mukunda Lal's destined Sadguru. With great love and affection, Sriyukteshvarji took Mukunda Lal to his Ranamahal residence. After they spoke for a while, Sriyukteshvarji came to know that Mukunda Lal was his guru-brother [fellow disciple of the same guru] Bhagabati Charan's son, and how and why Mukunda had come to Benares and all such things. Mukunda Lal beseeched him to please initiate him, receive him as his disciple and make him a sannyasi. Swamiji Maharaj assured him that initiation would certainly happen now, but this was not yet the time for sannyas. Mukunda had to finish other necessary work before taking sannyas; he had to receive a university degree first. Mukunda Lal did not like this proposition at all; he was determined that he had to become a sannyasi now; this is why he had left home and come here. Swamiji Maharaj said, "You have to become great. Of course you'll be a sannyasi but what will you be able to do by being a little weakling baba [sage]? You have to become like Swami Vivekananda. It is for this reason that you have to get a B.A. degree." The example of Swami Vivekananda stirred Mukunda's heart, because in those days all spiritual-minded, patriotic Indian youths' ideal was Mother India's valiant son Swami Vivekananda. Nevertheless, Mukunda again requested sannyas right then. He felt hesitation in going back and admitting defeat, after having left all of the complications of house and home. Sriyukteshvarji assured him that he would write to Mukunda's father and explain everything. Thus it was set that Mukunda would return home, go back to college and visit Sriyukteshvarji at Serampore [Srirampur]. Mukunda Lal went back to the Bharat Dharma Mahamandal ashram and told his friend Jitendra Lal about all that had happened and said, "Now we're free from here. Let's go home." He opened the container given by his mother and saw that the amulet was gone; it had done its work and had gone back to its original abode, evidencing that he had not made a mistake in recognition; he truly had found his Sadguru. Before going to Calcutta, first they went to Ananta Lal's home in Agra, where he had relocated from Calcutta. Ananta Lal again rebuked his spiritually-mad brother, but his brother remained unmoved, saying, "All is possible by God's

Grace." After arguing with him, Mukunda Lal made a bet with his brother and without taking a single penny, Mukunda and Jiten left for Vrindavan, and they toured Vrindavan in princely fashion and came back to Agra. Even the unbelieving Ananta Lal was astounded by this. Mukunda and Jiten then headed straight for Calcutta from Agra.

[*Translator's note: The statement within quotation marks is written in English in the original manuscript.]

Upon returning to Calcutta, instead of going back to the Metropolitan College, Mukunda Lal enrolled in the Scottish Church College. One day soon after this, he went to Swamiji Maharaj Sriyukteshvar Giriji in Serampore and received initiation from him into the practice of Kriya Yoga in the traditional way. Having fulfilled the greatest desire of the heart—having one's Sadguru—Mukunda Lal busied himself in his college studies as instructed by Sri Guru. However it was spiritual work that received more of his attention although he managed to be regularly present in class with books and papers. Whenever he found an opportunity, he would run to Sri Guru at Serampore. Mukunda Lal was a natural leader; thus within a short time, college-mates oriented towards higher things began to gather around and follow him. Manomohan Majumdar and the other follower-friends previously mentioned were of course there, but now there were new friends with spiritual inclinations. Among them was Basu Kumar Bagchi, the son of P.M. Bagchi from Shantipur of the Nadia district. Seeing Mukunda Lal's ever-joyful behavior, genuine affection towards friends, deep longing to live the spiritual life, intense devotion to Sri Guru and the great beings of the guru-parampara [spiritual lineage], and sometimes bearing witness to his extra-rational powers in certain situations, Mukunda Lal's friends and companions wholly took him up as their leader. Not only did the gatherings of spiritual discussions go on just as before, but visiting Sri Guru Maharaj with one or two friends at a time also became a regular thing. Mukunda Lal dove deeply into long sessions of Kriya sadhana; constantly with him like a shadow was Manomohan and now Basu Kumar as the third close-companion. Mukunda Lal taught Kriya to Manomohan and Basu Kumar. From very early on in childhood, Mukunda Lal was devoted to Mother Kali as his Divine Supreme Goddess; after his birth-mother passed away, he saw her as being one with the Divine Mother and received great energy and uplift from Her in that way. The other godman in his life was Paramguru Thakur [Lord] Sri Sri Shyama Charan Lahiri Mahasaya. The Universal Mother, Paramguru, and his own guru were the helmspersons of his life, the fulfillers of his destiny and his Supreme Shelter.

Studying at College and Being in the Company of Sri Guru

It has already been mentioned that Mukunda tried to be present in class
as much as possible. However, he always looked for an excuse to go to
Serampore. His uncle [younger brother of his father] Sri Sarada Charan
Ghosh, a prominent man in the field of law, lived in Serampore as a highly
respected member of the community. Thus, when it was necessary, there was
no problem with Mukunda's staying overnight in that town. In any case,
most of the time he stayed with Sri Guru himself. Whenever he would learn
any new wisdom or process regarding sadhana, he would return to Calcutta
and teach these things to the disciple-like Manomohan and Basu Kumar.
In this way, his role as a teacher went on unabated. They regularly practiced
Kriya, meditation and contemplation together. Although Manomohan had
known Mukunda longer than Basu Kumar, he was the youngest of the
three. Basu Kumar was not only of the same age as Mukunda Lal, he
was a schoolmate in the same class-year, highly intelligent, energetic and
physically very handsome. Gradually, Basu Kumar became Mukunda Lal's
favored one; it can even be said that they were seen by others as inseparable.
Manomohan remained as part of the triumvirate but he was considered third
in the hierarchy. Mukunda Lal became very drawn to Basu Kumar and Basu
Kumar's influence also began to show on him. All in all it can be said that
Mukunda Lal became more or less mesmerized with Basu Kumar's presence.
He also took both Basu Kumar and Manomohan many times to guru
Sriyukteshvarji. Gurudev was well aware of the relationships between the
three of them. Mukunda Lal was extremely feeling-oriented, a vessel of love,
uncomplicated, a natural sadhak and mad for spirituality; Basu Kumar was
steady, stoic, renunciate, analytical and intellectual; Manomohan was also
feeling-oriented, uncomplicated and renunciate and Mukunda Lal's shadow-
like follower. Although Mukunda Lal was very close to Basu Kumar, it seems
that he would sometimes say, "You [Basu Kumar] are extremely 'dry'! It is
with Manomohan that my destiny lies." The writer heard this directly from
Swami Satyanandaji's mouth. Also, Gurudev Sriyukteshvarji did not like
Mukunda Lal's excessive closeness with Basu Kumar, and Mukunda Lal
was aware of this himself. For this reason, whenever he had to carry out
a task that he knew would not be looked upon favorably by Gurudev but
had to do it because of Basu Kumar's persistent insistence, he would try to
do it without Gurudev knowing about it. But nothing remained hidden to
his omniscient Gurudev, especially when it concerned his Spirit-intoxicated
Mukunda, humanity's son. The writer came to know Gurudev's feelings
about this particular matter many years afterwards. It will be written about
later in its appropriate place and context.

Swami Sriyukteshvar Giriji Maharaj
("Swami Maharaj")

Meeting with Ram Gopal Majumdar, the sage of Ranarajpur

College life was more or less going along in an acceptable manner. Mukunda Lal was present in class most times but then again sometimes would not go. The habit of seeking the company of holy persons was still intensely alive in him. Usually he would tell Sri Guru about wanting to see some saint and go to such personages most of the time with Sri Guru's permission. However, some of the times he would go without telling his Gurudev, and when this would happen, Mukunda Lal would approach Sri Guru with trepidation, fearing that Gurudev may admonish him for his actions. But when it came to these matters, Gurudev never showed any signs of disapproval; instead, he behaved in a completely nonchalant manner, as if nothing had happened. Because of this Mukunda's reverence and devotion towards his Gurudev grew tremendously. The feeling of wanting to escape to the Himalayas still had not abated in him completely, but his heart did not want to leave his guru's side. Once he actually had asked permission from Sri Guru to go to the Himalayas; Gurudev neither forbade him nor outwardly expressed anything affirmative. At this time, Mukunda Lal did go away to have audience with a holy sage, but not in the Himalayas; it was in a village near Tarakeshvar, where he went to see Sri Sri Ram Gopal Majumdar of Ranarajpur. That was a wondrous experience for Mukunda Lal. He had heard about the advanced yogic achievements of the sage of Ranarajpur from his Sanskrit professor at Scottish Church College. This great yogi-saint was an eminent disciple of Yogiraj Sri Sri Lahiri Mahasaya. Mukunda Lal felt that instead of going to the Himalayas, it was more important to go and see this great being. Determined to find him, one day he took a train to the Tarakeshvar station. Ranarajpur was a few miles farther via a footpath. After asking around a bit, he began walking on that path. Everyone had said that it would be best to try to reach the village by nightfall. But no matter how far he went, when he would ask the passersby, they would tell him that he still had the same distance to go as he was told previously. The sense of distance in rural peoples—as far as miles and furlongs and such—is often very unreliable. Those who have traveled in the jungle areas of Chota Rampur—at least during the time before Independence—know this to be true. [Translator's note: Sri Sailendra Bejoy Dasgupta gives examples of confusing ideas of distance that are typical of the rural folk mentality in Bengal. Because of the colloquial terms used in this segment, the translator has tried to reword this segment in a way that can be understood by international readers. This segment is set off by "+" signs at its beginning and end.] + One mile remains "just a mile" even after traversing five miles. This is why experienced travelers of the jungle area sarcastically call "a mile" the "broken-branch mile." When one breaks off a young and thin branch from a tree and walks until the leaves become dry—until this time has passed one has not crossed the jungle's "just a mile" distance. + Mukunda Lal's situation was somewhat like this. He had been walking and walking, and evening was approaching, but he still had far to go before he would reach his destination. On top of this, he eventually found out that he was now traveling for a good long while on the wrong road, and the village was actually very far from where he had ended up at this point. Night was falling; there was not a soul around. What would he do now? Fortunately, he saw a bullock cart at a distance. Mukunda Lal approached the driver of the cart and asked him about some possible lodging for the night. The driver took pity on the young man and made arrangements for Mukunda Lal to spend the night at his home, which was a short distance from where they met. The next morning, after receiving directions to Ranarajpur once more, he again set out with haste. The sun was rising higher and higher in the sky; there was nothing but desolate countryside all around; Ranarajpur was still "a long way, over on the other side." When the sun was directly above his head and Mukunda Lal could barely keep going with heat, hunger, thirst and exhaustion, he saw a man far away who seemed to be walking directly towards him. As the man came closer, upon seeing his radiant, meditative and yogic eyes Mukunda Lal knew instantly that this stranger was Sri Ram Gopal Majumdar himself. After introductions and ceremonially taking the dust off of the sage's feet, Mukunda Lal followed the saint and finally reached his destination. The Shakti-endowed yogi must have come to know through his yogic powers that a young Kriya yogi-sadhak was coming to see him and was suffering on the road after going in the wrong direction. The residence of Ram Gopalji was nothing but a little hut with palm leaves for a roof. The room was more or less bare; there was a blanket for sleeping, a seat on the floor for meditation and a few utensils for cooking. Immediately upon their arrival, Sri Ram Gopal made Mukunda a drink of sweetened lime juice and water, relieving his thirst and tiredness. Later he prepared some "khichuri" [blend of rice and pulse] by his own hands and satisfied Mukunda's hunger. Sri Ram Gopal spread out a blanket for Mukunda and told him to get some sleep. But sleep would not come. He kept seeing a radiant glow all around, whether it was with his eyes closed or open, but there was no lighted lamp. Sometime in the deep night the great sage said, "Now go to sleep." Mukunda did then go to sleep, but Ram Gopalji remained seated on his meditation seat. In the morning, when Mukunda was bidding farewell, Sri Ram Gopal asked Mukunda to stand in front of him for a short while, and then they took their goodbyes. Mukunda Lal suddenly realized that within this momentary period, a pain that he had had in his back for quite a long time had instantly vanished. Later, Mukunda Lal came to find out that Sri Ram Gopal lived for many years without sleep; he was absorbed in meditation almost ceaselessly.

After returning home, Mukunda Lal went to see Sri Guru in Serampore at the first opportunity he got, but with some fear, because Sri Guru had not outwardly given him permission to go away. However, when they met, Gurudev welcomed Mukunda in his usual affectionate manner. And Gurudev also expressed joy upon hearing Mukunda's descriptive telling of his experience with Sri Ram Gopal Majumdar in Ranarajpur.

Experiencing Sri Guru's Divine Grace in Puri

In the following year, when college was on hiatus during the holy holiday season, Mukunda Lal spent practically the entire holiday with Gurudev in his Puri ashram. This was the first time he had spent this amount of uninterrupted time with his guru. During this period, Mukunda Lal bore direct witness to Gurudev's unimaginable yogic powers and the unfathomable depths of his wisdom. Among many divine and supernatural experiences, one particular event seems appropriate to elucidate here. While Mukunda Lal stayed with Gurudev, he had a great deal of time and opportunity available—morning, dusk, night—for the regular practice of Kriya Yoga, deep meditation and sadhana. One late afternoon, when Mukunda Lal had sat for meditation, Gurudev called him from the veranda. At first, Mukunda Lal did not want to get up from his seat of meditation. He heard the voice of Gurudev again, this time far more severe. He quickly got up and went and stood before his guru on the veranda. Gurudev immediately touched him on the forehead and chest and Mukunda Lal lost all physical consciousness. It seemed that he had become one with the Infinite. The ocean far away, the waves of the ocean—he could see everything. He saw that he pervaded everything. This was an incredible, indescribable experience. He had no knowledge of the amount of time that had passed while he was in this state. When Gurudev again touched his forehead and chest, he returned to his normal state of consciousness. Overcome with reverence, devotion and gratitude, Mukunda Lal was about to fall in full prostration at his guru's feet, when he heard Sriyukteshvarji's stern order, "Go quickly and sweep the veranda. Then we must take a walk by the seaside." Mukunda Lal was heartbroken when he heard this. In place of expressing his being overcome with devotion at his guru's feet was now this order to do something as mundane as sweeping! Even in 1935, when Yoganandaji described this event, he still could not hide his heartbrokenness of that time. Who knows—perhaps this was the type of discipline he needed. Perhaps this type of dry physical task was assigned so that this ecstatically prone "child of humanity" would not float away with the buoyancy of Divine Ecstasy and forget the mundane. Among all of the disciples, Mukunda Lal was exceptional in that he was witness to more of the rare outward expressions of Gurudev's tender heart. About this, the world-conquering Swami Yogananda said later, "I have never seen a more wise and powerful yogi such as Swamiji [Sriyukteshvarji], but if he had just showed a little more of the loving feeling and sweetness in his heart, it would have been so nice. He was a bit too tough in his ways." As Mukunda Lal held Sriyukteshvarji in the highest spiritual place, he feared Gurudev terribly when it came to practical matters of daily life. His behavior towards Gurudev always was like that of a child, even after Yoganandaji attained worldwide eminence. At the time when Yoganandaji stayed in India during the years 1935-36, this writer himself was a direct witness to Yoganandaji's "desperate" condition; like a schoolboy who had come to his teacher without having studied, he would sit in front of Sriyukteshvarji in this kind of apprehensive state. In any case—with the regular company of Gurudev, the practice of Kriya Yoga, meditation, devotionals, spiritual discussions, being guru-like for his friends and follower-companions, and sometimes playing hooky from school for these reasons—the days moved forward like this. The I.A. examinations were soon approaching, but Mukunda Lal had not prepared at all for the tests. Where was the time—or desire—to read and study? All of his college-mates at that time would spend most of their free time intensely preparing for the exams. Whenever he would even think about the tests he would become terribly frightened; he would have been extremely happy not to have to sit for the tests. Everyone else would forgive him. But Gurudev?!! Oh no, there was no hope of any deliverance from him on this matter; he was a "very hard nut to crack"! Also, it was because of Gurudev's instructions that Mukunda Lal had re-enrolled in college and, as per Gurudev's directive from quite a while ago, he absolutely had to receive a B.A. degree. But the boat was about to sink! Who could save it from drowning now? What other recourse was there for Mukunda Lal other than relying on Sri Guru's Grace? At that time, Gurudev was in Puri, staying for the time being in his ashram there. Without any other way out, Mukunda Lal hurried off to see his guru in Puri. Upon hearing about his disciple's situation regarding preparations for the exams, Gurudev solemnly said, "Go back home. Work as hard as you can and get ready for the tests. Do not waste even a single moment." Mukunda Lal had thought that perhaps after hearing about his predicament Gurudev would be a bit sympathetic towards him and perhaps he would advise Mukunda to not sit for the exams this year and prepare for next year. But alas, his guru was a "very hard nut to crack"! To expect any coddling from him for these kinds of weaknesses was useless. And Mukunda of course had to follow his guru's orders. He returned to Calcutta in this crestfallen state, and putting his faith fully upon Sadguru, immersed himself into studying day and night for the exams. He had not even a drop of faith in his own ability to pass the tests; his sole reliance was his all-beneficent savior Gurudev. In due time, the exams were held and completed. The announcement of the results showed that Mukunda Lal had passed.

Studying for the B.A. Degree in a College in Serampore and Traveling to Kashmir with Sri Guru

The other shore was not yet in sight; Mukunda Lal still had to finish the B.A. degree. He felt that it could not go on like this any more. If he had to continue with college then he had to enroll in some college close to Gurudev's residence. This running back and forth between Calcutta and Serampore to have only a little time in Gurudev's company—this situation had to change. Mukunda Lal proposed to Gurudev that if he had to study for the B.A., then he wanted to do so at a college in Serampore, and he prayed for Gurudev's permission. Hearing this proposal, Gurudev smiled within and said that he would write to Mukunda's father Bhagabati Charan and organize everything. Gurudev of course knew what his spiritual son's real intentions were. Arrangements were then made for Mukunda Lal to begin the B.A. program at the Wesleyan Mission College in Serampore and to stay at his previously mentioned uncle Sarada Charan's home. Sarada Charan's house was on Rani Road (presently Netaji Subhas Chandra Bose Road), only two or three minutes from Gurudev's house. Sarada Charan set up separate quarters for Mukunda in which he could live and study in privacy. Mukunda Lal was extremely happy; now it was very easy to be in Gurudev's company daily. However, within a short time, he came to know that his father and aunt back home were being informed of his activities, and that his father was finding out that Mukunda was spending most of his time with his guru instead of studying! In order to keep an eye on him, the pragmatically experienced Bhagabati Charan took measures to have Mukunda's younger brother Sananda Lal to also stay and study with him. Mukunda Lal began to think of a way out of this distressing situation. And a resolution was found. It was arranged for Mukunda to stay in the college hostel itself. Now there was no hindrance in going to see Gurudev. And this happened not only during off-hours; many times he skipped class to spend time with Gurudev, if not every day, then certainly very regularly. Mukunda Lal was now like a free bird. However, Sananda Lal tried to keep track of his elder brother's whereabouts, and he reported whatever he found out to his father. But there was nothing more that could be done about his spiritually-mad son; Bhagabati Charan had to resign to be content with Mukunda Lal studying for the B.A. at all. The result of staying at the hostel was this: not only were classes skipped from time to time, but Mukunda Lal would not even come back to the hostel some nights, spending the time instead with Gurudev. It was at this time that Mukunda Lal experienced the touch of the outwardly stern Sriyukteshvarji's tender heart within. Among the many disciples of Sriyukteshvarji, only Mukunda Lal had the fortune of experiencing this very secret and unknown side of Gurudev's nature. When Yoganandaji returned to India in 1935, he spoke of two such incidents; it is possible that these accounts came out of his mouth when he was not being attentive about guarding his speech. Once Swamiji Maharaj Sriyukteshvarji fell very ill; there was tremendous pain in his head. Mukunda Lal was tending to his Gurudev. At some point he held Sriyukteshvarji's head on his lap and was stroking his Gurudev's forehead in order to relieve the pain. At this time, Swamiji Maharaj spoke out, "If I ever fall, will you be able to take me up in your lap like this?!" When the world-renowned Yoganandaji was recounting this event, his eyes welled up with tears. And it seems there was another time when Gurudev said to him, "After you came, any desire I may have had to marry again completely disappeared." When recounting this expression of Gurudev's love towards him, Yoganandaji had his head bowed and was lost in the absorption of love for his Gurudev. The writer has heard from Swami Satyanandaji: it seems that Mukunda Lal used to whisper in the ears of his dearest friends and followers Basu Kumar and Manomohan, "The Beloved is the Supreme Guru." It is very possible that he used to state this maxim of conduct to them after experiencing Gurudev's expression of Divine Love. To see this kind of depth and beauty in a guru-disciple relationship is unquestionably very rare.

During one of the summer holidays at this time in Serampore, Mukunda Lal made plans to visit Kashmir with some of his friends and Gurudev. Gurudev agreed to go. Entreating his father, Mukunda Lal was able to procure the money needed to fund the cost of the trip and gather the required necessities such as railway passes etc. The date for travel was then set. On that date and time, all of his friends assembled at the train station; it was planned previously that Mukunda Lal would bring Swamiji Maharaj to the station. A short while before leaving the house, Swamiji Maharaj said that they should leave just a little later. A few moments after that Mukunda Lal was suddenly struck with a combination of diarrhea and vomiting, and he fell terribly ill. Gurudev hurriedly began to tend to him. His friends waited at the station and when they did not see Swamiji Maharaj or Mukunda after a long period, they went to Swamiji Maharaj's house. They were stunned to see their dear friend's condition. A physician was called, and after being tenderly taken care of by his Gurudev and friends, Mukunda Lal recovered his health, much to the relief of everyone. Yoganandaji used to say that Gurudev knew beforehand that he would be stricken like that at that time and that is why Swamiji Maharaj said that they should leave a little later. After Mukunda Lal's recovery, Swamiji Maharaj himself set the new date for traveling to Kashmir, and soon enough, everyone again became excited about going to the land that was known as "bhusvarga" [heaven on earth]. The train journey took them through stops at Simla and Rawalpindi. Everyone was captivated by Simla's beautiful scenery. From Rawalpindi the travelers took horse-drawn carriages to Srinagar, the capital city of Kashmir. No one could hold back their joy upon seeing the loveliness of this "heaven on earth." After spending a few days and seeing all the major sights, they also experienced the attraction for which Kashmir is well known—residing in one of the famous houseboats in Srinagar. Finally, Mukunda Lal and his friends had to leave for home. Swamiji Maharaj would stay in Kashmir for a few more days with two assistants at his side. When they were saying their goodbyes, Gurudev told Mukunda Lal that most likely a dangerous illness would befall him [Sriyukteshvarji] very soon; it could even take his life. Mukunda Lal was absolutely beside himself upon hearing this. He cried out to Gurudev that there for no reason whatsoever could he cast off his body now, and that he had to promise this before Mukunda and his friends would leave for home. The supremely compassionate Sriyukteshvarji softened at the heartbreaking plea of his love-immersed disciple and assured him, "As you wish, so shall it be my wish also." Feeling solace in Gurudev's binding words of reassurance, Mukunda Lal returned to Calcutta with his friends. But within just a few days, news arrived saying that Gurudev was extremely ill in Kashmir. In desperation, Mukunda Lal said to his father that he immediately needed to write a telegram to his Gurudev. In the wire, Mukunda beseechingly reminded Gurudev of his promise, and begged him to not even think about leaving his body in any way whatsoever. Swamiji Maharaj recovered a few days later and returned home from Kashmir.

Receiving the B.A. Degree

The beginning of the year 1914 came and the B.A. examinations were also at hand. One day, Gurudev asked how the preparations for the tests were going. Mukunda Lal dried up inside upon hearing this question. How could he possibly tell Gurudev the truth? Somehow he answered, "Preparations are happening." But far from preparation even being mentioned, just thinking that he would have to sit for the exams made Mukunda Lal completely discombobulated. Gurudev asked the same question another day and although not sounding completely sheepish and helpless, Mukunda was not very convincing in his answer. When Gurudev asked a third time on another day, Mukunda said with trepidation, "I'm thinking that maybe I won't sit for the tests this year. I'll prepare well for the exams next year and take them then." Upon hearing this answer, Swamiji Maharaj stared directly at Mukunda and gravely said, "You have to take the exams this year and you also have to pass. I won't hear another word. Now go. Study and prepare." There was no possible way Mukunda Lal could say anything in response to this, and neither did he have the courage to do so. With his head lowered like a sacrificial animal, he returned to the college hostel. But before he left, Gurudev named a certain classmate and told Mukunda to discuss and get advice on the subjects from this student and to study with him as well. Swamiji Maharaj had actually heard about this excellent student previously from Mukunda Lal himself. After returning to the students' quarters, Mukunda met that classmate friend, revealed his sorry predicament, and asked him for his help in studying. The friend enthusiastically agreed and said that he would help in every way he could. Steadying himself, Mukunda Lal began to study for the exams. His friend tried to help as much as possible. But the more he studied, the more discouraged Mukunda Lal became. It became obvious that however far he felt that he had fallen behind, he was actually much, much farther behind than where he thought he was. It was nothing but misguided bravado to even imagine sitting for the exams in this state. But how could he explain this to his leonine Gurudev? Thinking about that regal, fiery form made Mukunda cringe with apprehension. He resigned himself to whatever fate had written; he had to take the tests; there was no way out. He immersed himself day and night in study, but there was not even a glint of light showing any sort of progress. The examination days had almost arrived. One day right at this time, Mukunda was walking on the road with books in hand when a piece of paper—a page from a notebook—floated past him. It was bouncing and rolling—moving away slowly on the road ahead. He quickly went and grabbed the paper and saw that on it were some test questions from one of his lines of study. Chills ran through him. Saying "whatever fate may hold," he decided that he would just prepare for those questions alone. Those questions happened to be for the subject in which he was the most behind and which he feared the most. He returned to the students' quarters and carefully began to prepare for all of the questions on that paper. Finally, the first day of the exams arrived. Taking blessings and the dust off of the feet of Sri Guru on his head, Mukunda Lal sat for the exams, relying on nothing but Sri Guru. But he was amazed and overjoyed to find out that most of the questions for his most feared subject happened to be printed versions of the questions on the questionnaire he had found lying around on the road. Happily, he wrote down what he had studied. He tried his best on the other days with the other tests as well. But Mukunda Lal felt that there was no hope of succeeding without his Gurudev's Grace. The results were eventually announced. When he saw that his name was printed among those who had passed, he could not find any reason for this being possible other than his Gurudev's divine powers and his infinite Grace towards his disciple. Mukunda Lal had fulfilled his spiritual teacher's wish and was now the recipient of a B.A. degree! Dancing with joy, he went first to his Gurudev, prostrated to him and presented him with this wonderful news. And no matter whom Mukunda Lal met to tell them of this joyous happening, right at the very beginning he would say that this achievement had absolutely nothing to do with his own abilities; it was possible only by the might of his supremely compassionate Guru's immeasurable yogic powers. Till his last days, in every opportunity he found, Yoganandaji spoke of passing his B.A. exams as an example of his Shaktiendowed Gurudev's yogic powers.

CHAPTER 2
The Beginnings of Service

Founding the First Calcutta Yogoda Satsanga Center in a Shantytown Thatched Hut

After receiving the B.A. degree, because of requests by his friends and his father, Mukunda Lal enrolled for the M.A. program as well. But he stopped going to the university after just a few days. It was at this time that his future life of service would be set in motion. It can be said this was the beginning of becoming the "engine of the future," as was prophesied by the Supreme Yogi and Holy of Holies, Paramguru Lahiri Baba. The two follower-friends Basu Kumar and Manomohan were overjoyed to now have their leader in Calcutta all the time. Manomohan had passed his matriculation exams and had just enrolled in college, and Basu Kumar was enrolled for M.A. studies. The three of them again began to do sadhana together, along with performing devotionals and having spiritual discussions. And now, a desire to have an "ashram" of their own arose in Mukunda. But from where would the funds come? His father was taking care of his regular needs. Mukunda could not possibly ask him to fund this kind of whim on top of the support he was already providing. The prayer room at Tulsi Narayan's house was not that appropriate, and it was not private or quiet enough. After a long search, a place was found in a shantytown of Muraripukur by the canal in north Calcutta. It was nothing but a shack in a shantytown, but still it was their own! It was in this new "ashram" that the three friends practiced Kriya Yoga, meditation and devotionals together, and they also began to hold gatherings of spiritual discussions from time to time. Mukunda Lal and his two follower-friends were extremely happy at having founded this first "ashram." No one—not even Mukunda Lal himself—could imagine at that time that this totally unremarkable and seemingly insignificant "ashram" would grow into an immense world-wide institution as the primary example of Mukunda Lal's—later Yoganandaji's—achievements, and would evolve into a shining beacon of the ancient spiritual wisdom of India.

Refusal of the Allure of a Lucrative Job

However, Mukunda's extremely wise and life-seasoned father Bhagabati Charan did not remain a silent witness. This highly able, vigilant man with great insight in human nature was well aware of his son's tendencies since birth and was trying to find some way to make Mukunda Lal into a householder. Being the tremendously adept and powerful personal secretary of the Agent of the Bengal-Nagpur Railway Company, this great achiever secretly received permission from the Agent to create a high and very well-paid position within the rail company for his B.A. graduate son. Along with the railway, this company also earned tens of millions of rupees from the manufacturing and sale of equipment for businesses. The main yard of the company was in Kharagpur, which is also where the deals and shipments were made for the aforementioned equipment. But there was only one managing director of operations for all the work in this area, a controller who carried out his duties from the company's central offices in Calcutta. Stating that there was a need for more organization in this massively important division of the firm, Bhagabati Charan convinced the Agent to create a position of Deputy Controller for the Kharagpur affairs. The monthly salary for this position was six hundred rupees. How attractive a salary this was for that time can only be understood in comparison to salaries in other high level positions; for example, the monthly income for an I.C.S. officer of the Government of India at that time was two hundred fifty rupees. One day the astute Bhagabati Charan struck up a conversation with his son about the goings on at the ashram. After listening for a while he said, "Because you're having to do this by begging, having to run this ashram by getting whatever you can from begging, I've found a very well paid job for you. You can do whatever you like from that salary; make and run an ashram, or spend that money on whatever you like. I don't need any money; so you don't have to worry about giving even a cent of that salary to me." Mukunda Lal's clever father had the contract papers for his son with him, already signed by the Agent, which he now put in Mukunda Lal's hands. Mukunda was astounded at the seeing the amount of the monthly salary written in the contract. How much effort they had to make to just make ends meet at their poor ashram! Although he found the idea of working at a job for someone else an absolutely repulsive thing, he could not reject his father's proposition outright, especially on account of the salary. He said that he needed to think about it for a few days. He returned hastily to the ashram in Muraripukur and the three friends began to deeply analyze the proposition. Seeing that the salary was beyond anything that any of them could have thought up, all three were at a loss for what to do. It would make things so much easier if this kind of money came in every month. But alas, it had to end up like this! Taking a job after all?! All three were united at heart; they were true friends; they were tied together by a vow that they would formally take sannyas; they were only youths, not mature about the world; it was indeed a difficult decision for them to make. But the main character in this particular situation was Mukunda Lal; thus he was the one who had to make the decision. The three friends stayed up all night discussing the matter. Finally, Mukunda came to a resolution and made his decision. He said that no matter how attractive the money is, if one steps in that trap once, there is no way of escaping it. But it would not be right to just throw away this much money. "The snake must be killed, but without breaking the stick." If some kind of way could be found to achieve this, it would be the ideal thing. And such a way was found. Mukunda Lal's cousin, Serampore's Uncle Sarada's son Prabhas Chandra was a diligent B.A. graduate, sweet in behavior, physically very attractive and very sharp in intellect. And he was also a true follower-devotee of elder cousin-brother Mukunda Lal. Although in the B.A. exams he placed second with honors in philosophy, it was in the second class. Prabhas Chandra's classmate friend Saroj Das—who would later become the head of the philosophy department of a university and a venerated professor as well—placed first in first class. Feeling angry and dejected at not being placed in first class, Prabhas Chandra decided to not pursue the M.A. And Mukunda Lal decided that he would tell his father to give that job to Prabhas Chandra, with the condition that Mukunda's cousin would freely donate funds from his salary to help the ashram. This decision was satisfactory to all three friends. Mukunda took this proposition to his father and said that Prabhas Chandra was far more qualified for this type of work, and besides that, he did not at all want to take up a regular job himself. Mukunda Lal requested his father to please consider this option. Bhagabati Charan knew his son's nature and mentality very well, and on the outside at least, he said with anger and disappointment, "All right then. Just go and do whatever you want." He had had to flatter and indulge his Agent boss quite a lot to be able to create this position in the name of his son. But now his son was completely against taking this job; how could he face the Agent now? And he also had to acknowledge that Mukunda Lal's statement was correct: Prabhas Chandra actually was a much better candidate for the position than Mukunda—in every way. Besides that, after creating a job with this kind of salary and prestige, it would also not sit well if someone outside the family got the position. After mulling it over for a while, Bhagabati Charan somehow, with great effort, made the Agent understand this situation and thereafter hired Prabhas Chandra for the position. Getting a job with that kind of salary with a railway company at such a young age was unthinkable in those days. But because of Mukunda Lal's love and compassion, Prabhas Chandra had just such a position, and his facial hair was not even like a full grown adult's at this time. Even in later years there was no sign of any change in the love that Yoganandaji and Prabhas Chandra felt for each other. Prabhas Chandra and his virtuous wife were an ideal couple; however they had no children. His younger brother Prakash Chandra's son and daughter were looked upon as children of both brothers. Both of their wives were also very close and were there for each other in every way. Elder stepbrother Prasad Chandra Ghosh also held a high position with a rail company—the E.I. Railway. Prabhas Chandra continuously gave a great deal of financial support to Yoganandaji's ashramic work; he even donated his paternal home in Serampore. When Yoganandaji established his Yogoda Satsanga Society in India, he assigned the position of "Saha Sabhapati" [Co-Director or Co-Chairman] to Prabhas Chandra. Even before Bhagabati Charan retired, Prabhas Chandra proved himself as an indispensable and highly respected member of the company. And this was not at all an easy achievement at that time, because in those days, all of the rail companies' highest positions were taken by British personnel, and there was a monopoly held on the jobs just under them by the "anglo-Indian" collective.

Taking the Vow of Sannyas

In any case, after all of this, Mukunda Lal made up his mind that he was not going to wait any longer; it was time to take the formal vow of sannyas [renunciation/renunciate monkhood]. When he expressed this desire to Gurudev, Sriyukteshvarji happily agreed. Mukunda Lal now presented himself by his sannyas name—Swami Yogananda. Immediately after having become a sannyasi, a desire to make new efforts at service dawned in him. Of course, first and foremost, he would put his whole being into the work of his guru's Yogoda Satsanga Sabha. Up to now, the main center for the Calcutta-based part of this organization was in Kidderpore [Khidirpur], a branch which had some highly advanced disciples of Sriyukteshvarji in attendance, such as Amulya Charan Santra, Amulya Das, Charu Chandra Mitra and writer Roy Bahadur Atul Chandra Choudhury. Now, Swami Yogananda set up another center in Calcutta, comprised mostly of educated youths who were disciple-devotees. The elder Kriyavans in Kidderpore were delighted at the efforts of this energetic, young yogi guru-brother. The Kidder-pore Kriyavans were well aware of Yogananda's father Bhagabati Charan's renowned status, because the B.N. Railway's main place of operations was in Kidderpore itself. These great spiritual luminaries welcomed Bhagabati Charan's virtuous renunciate son with loving hearts and open arms. It is important to mention here that there was someone that the Kriyavans of Kidderpore held as a kind of leader—Sri Motilal Mukhopadhyay of Serampore-Chatra. Moti Babu lived in Kidderpore because of his job and was one who encouraged many seekers to receive Kriya Yoga initiation from Gurudev. Among the guru-brothers [in this case, the disciples of Sriyukteshvarji] Moti Babu was considered most senior and in 1902, it was to him that Sriyukteshvarji bestowed the title of "sampadak" [executive or director] of Swamiji Maharaj's newly created Satsanga Sabha. The new center in Calcutta was set up in a one-floor house adjacent to Tulsi Narayan's family home on Raja Dinendra Street. Acharya Ashutosh Shastri Mahasaya was often present at the events held at this center.

Sri Motilal Mukhopadhyay ("Moti Babu") of Serampore
A revered disciple of Sriyukteshvar Giriji Maharaj

Journey to Japan

However, Yogananda was not completely content with only doing this kind of work. He wished to do something big, and for this purpose, a desire to go abroad began to dominate his thoughts. Rare indeed was an Indian who was not as "proud as proud can be" of Swami Vivekenanda's accomplishments—the first victory for India's spirituality via his travels in America and India gaining respect throughout the world. Yogananda also wanted to follow in Vivekananda's footsteps in a similar way. He set it in his mind to go to Japan to spread the wisdom and teachings of yoga. In those days, Japan was sort of a place of pilgrimage for independence-hungry Indians. It was Japan that first proved to the West that in no way or degree were Asians any weaker than Westerners in prowess, valor or skill in any area of productivity. The astounding battle at Port Arthur had become a sort of symbol. All Indian youths knew that Swami Vivekananda had said that the city of Yokohama was like a paradise on earth. For all such young Indians, traveling and seeing Japan was the same as going on a great pilgrimage. Yogananda decided that he would go and see this dreamland of a nation. The year was 1916; he was twenty-three years old. Yogananda boarded an eastbound ship, crossed the Sea of China to the Pacific Ocean and eventually arrived in the city of Kobe. He was highly impressed by the cleanliness and orderliness of the city. However, he became absolutely disillusioned by the societal behavior of the people. He had believed the type of cultural and societal behavior by which he was brought up since birth to be the foundation of his life, and the norms and mores of this land seemed to be in conflict with his ideals. Yogananda was mentally distressed. He thus concluded that it was actually better to leave this inappropriate atmosphere. After just a few days of being in Japan, he returned on an India-bound ocean-liner. There were two significant events related to the Japan journey—the creation of a manuscript by Yoganandaji while on the ship and the establishment of close friendships with a couple of the passengers on board. The manuscript was later published in the United States as "Science of Religion," and this was the very first book he composed. Among the passengers on board, one was Dr. Satyendra Nath Mitra, who became very drawn to Kriya Yoga after conversing with Yoganandaji, and upon his return to India, Dr. Mitra received Kriya Yoga initiation from Swamiji Maharaj Sriyukteshvar Giri. The second significant passenger was Captain Rashid from an eminent family in the Indian city of Bombay. He had Western blood in him from both sides of his family. Very spiritual-minded, intelligent and open-hearted, this young man received Kriya Yoga initiation from Yoganandaji himself. Although he was Muslim by birth and family, his perspective was very open and he carried a lively and uplifted attitude in work and dealings with others. He had traveled to Europe, America and other countries since he was very young and he moved in the most exclusive and highest circles of society in every place. When Yoganandaji was facing many sorts of difficulties in America, an unexpected meeting occurred in the United States between him and Captain Rashid, and Captain Rashid took up the responsibility for setting up an organization there. Helping Swamiji substantially and in many ways, Captain Rashid was invaluable to Swamiji being established successfully in America.

Founding the Brahmacharya Vidyalaya

After returning to India from Japan, back together with friend-followers Basu Kumar and Manomohan, Yogananda again dived fully into his previous work with the Yogoda Satsanga Sabha. A short while afterwards, upon reading and hearing about the world-renowned Nobel-laureate Rabindranath Tagore's Shantiniketan Ashram, where modern academic education was being disseminated in an ideal and natural atmosphere like the days of yore, a desire arose in him to establish an ashram-school similar to that. He also came to know from Gurudev about the ideal kind of "guru-kula" [guru-disciple lineage] based "brahmacharya vidyalaya"* that needed to be established at this time and received Gurudev's advice on its philosophy and mode of operation. Yoganandaji made up his mind that he would found another "brahmacharya vidyalaya" besides Shantiniketan, one which was more traditional and more oriented towards the "guru-kula" ideals in its philosophy than Shantiniketan. But because of a lack of finances, the possibility of realizing this vision was weak at best, and finding a way to recruit students was yet another problem. There was an Oriya** boy who had come to Calcutta to find means to make a livelihood, and he was hired as a cook at Yoganandaji's small ashram. This boy could play "khol" [a type of barrel drum] very well and played the drum when devotional songs were sung during the weekly spiritual gatherings. This very intelligent and devotion-oriented youth, named Sujodhan Das was the one with whom the imagined "brahmacharya vidyalaya" was begun. It was this boy who would later be known to all the students at the Brahmacharya Vidyalaya as "Sujodhan-da" [elder brother Sujodhan].

[*Translator's note: "Brahmacharya vidyalaya" in the generic sense means: an academically oriented school/college with an emphasis on studying while observing certain codes of living—including chastity, spiritual reverence, morality, social service etc.—during the time of studentship. Later, Yoganandaji's school would use "Brahmacharya Vidyalaya" as its official and registered name.]

[**Translator's note: "Oriya"—person from the province of Orissa.]

The Maharaja of Kashim Bazar was renowned for his generous support of charitable work throughout India. This great man had once hidden Lord Clive in his house and saved the nobleman from being attacked and killed by mutinous soldiers. Manindra Chandra Nandi inherited his wealth and historically famous business empire from his maternal aunt, the Maharani [queen] Swarnamayi, and was subsequently bestowed the title of "maharaja." By God's Infinite Compassion, this great man of such immense wealth did not spend his finances in the superficial enjoyment of worldly pleasures like other maharajas. His nature was such that he took it as his life's purpose to use his fortune for good works for the people of the country. It is very rare in India nowadays to see anyone like this freely giving and generous man. There were very few institutions or programs of higher culture—no matter what the field—which were not touched by his beneficent hands or the aid of his influence and power, whether they were academic and scientific institutions, or establishments related to social work and art. Maharaja Bahadur [Maharaja of Kashim Bazar] was Vaishnav [worshipper of Vishnu], and his generosity in the area of the religious and spiritual affairs of the Hindus was known to all. One day, it dawned on Yogananda that he would like to see the Maharaja and ask him for his partnership and help in establishing the Brahmacharya Vidyalaya. Thus, on an auspicious date, he went to the Maharaja's residence in Calcutta and was able to have an audience with him. After introductions, when the Maharaja heard Yogananda's proposition, he looked silently at Yoganandaji for a short while and said, "You are God-sent.* During the last few days, I had also been thinking about establishing just such an ashram-school." It was as if they both were cut from the same mold as visionaries—a perfect fit of gem and gold. Yogananda let the Maharaja know that he had already begun a very small version of the Brahmacharya Vidyalaya with his friend-followers in Calcutta. Very happy at hearing this, the Maharaja asked Swamiji to prepare and present to him a document outlining the mission, description and plan of operations for the ashram school as soon as possible.

[*Translator's note: The phrase "You are God-sent" is in English in the original Bengali manuscript.]

Overjoyed, Yogananda returned to the tiny ashram-hut in Muraripukur and told Basu Kumar and Manomohan the exciting news. The three friends were ecstatic. Now, first and foremost was the preparation of a detailed description of the goals and methods of the school and arranging for the Maharaja to have a look at the efforts—albeit miniscule in scale—they had made already. The responsibility of writing the description was put on Basu Kumar because he was considered to be the best in the area of academic studies—most probably passed the M.A. by this time—and was the clearest thinker. Yogananda organized a gathering to welcome the Maharaja to see what they had begun as an example of the brahmacharya vidyalaya to come. The detailed proposal was finished and Basu Kumar delivered it to the Maharaja by his own hand. Upon reading the outlined plans, Maharaja Bahadur became extremely interested and said that he would like to see the ashram-school that had already been begun, small or not. Yogananda was preparing of course for just such an event, but one uncomfortable thing was that the total studentship of their school amounted to only one—Sujodhan. Some others had to be called in to represent themselves as brahmachari-students, at least for that day in front of the Maharaja. Among them was Yogananda's youngest brother Bishnu Charan and Manomohan's third brother Khireshmohan. Giving them some quick training in reciting sacred Sanskrit verses and clothing each of them in yellow garments, these youths were dressed up as little "brahmacharis" [chaste monks]. In the welcome committee were of course Tulsi Narayan and other such regular attendees; Acharya Ashutosh Shastri Mahasaya was one among the elders present. With the clarion call of conch shells, Maharaja Bahadur was welcomed and ushered in. The gathering took place in the one-floor cottage adjacent to Tulsi Narayan's family home. After the children recited sacred Sanskrit verses with palms in prayerful gesture, there was devotional singing and chanting. The virtue-minded Maharaja was enchanted by seeing the brahmachari-garbed youths, and was very pleased at hearing the recitation of sacred verses and devotional singing. He enthusiastically promised to take up the financial responsibility for the establishing and daily running of a brahma-charya vidyalaya. Seeing this extraordinary and unimaginable way by which his vision became fulfilled, Yogananda became overcome with joy, as he acknowledged the unseen hand of God and the Masters of his lineage behind it all.

First Establishment of School in Dihika—Relocating Later to Ranchi

In the district of Burdwan [Bardhoman], on the banks of the Damodar river, in lovely and serene setting in a village named Dihika, there was a landowner's office-house belonging to the princely estate of the Maharaja of Kashim Bazar. Maharaja Bahadur had the edifice repainted, cleaned up the land on which it was situated and added other rooms/cottages as was necessary, and handed over the entire property to Yoganandaji for the establishment of the brahmacharya vidyalaya. Taking Gurudev Swamiji Maharaj Sriyukteshvarji's advice and on an auspicious date chosen by Sriyukteshvarji himself—on the 22nd of March in 1917 of the Christian year, 12th of Chaitra in the Bengali calendar—on the Great Spring Equinox, the Brahmacharya Vidyalaya was founded on this very property. The official patron was of course the previously mentioned Maharaja of Kashim Bazar, Manindra Chandra Nandi

Bahadur. Many personages of noble repute were in attendance on that day of founding. Many people also came from Asansol. The heads of school naturally were Yogananda, Basu Kumar and Manomohan. To give them and show his enthusiastic support, Acharya Ashutosh Shastri Mahasaya was also present. Manomohan still had not finished his college studies at that time. Thus, the faculty of the school was comprised of Yogananda as principal/ director, Basu Kumar as headmaster and a local colleague as another teacher. Shastri Mahasaya resided in the ashram as spiritual teacher, teaching the students on the virtuous aspects of living. It was in this very place—meaning the ashram-school in Dihika—where Yogananda initiated Basu Kumar into the path of sannyas and gave him his new name—Swami Dhirananda. The Brahmacharya Vidyalaya began with only six students in residence. However, this number quietly began to grow. At that time, there were only two ashram-schools of this type in Bengal—one was the Shantiniketan Vidyalaya and the other was this Brahmacharya Vidyalaya in Dihika. Shantiniketan was influenced by the openness of Rabindranath Tagore, leaning somewhat towards the philosophy of the Brahmo Samaj,* and most of its students were from wealthy families. The Dihika Brahmacharya Vidyalaya was founded upon the Hindu "guru-kula" ideals, and was very attractive to conservative and middle class parents. Thus, the good reputation of this ashram-school began to spread all over, and along with that the number of enrollees also began to increase greatly, and problems with the allotment of space for the school began to be seen. At this time, Maharaja Manindra Chandra himself came to visit the school, and was very satisfied upon seeing the program at work. Swamiji Maharaj Sriyukteshvarji also came to see the ashram once. When Yogananda heard that Sriyukteshvarji was approaching the school, he became so overcome with joy that he darted out bare-chested and barefooted, and he more or less ran for quite a distance until he reached Sriyukteshvarji, welcomed him and escorted him to the ashram himself. This was a very special opportunity for Yoganandaji to show his first creation and the first big accomplishment in his life to the one who was his teacher of teachers.

[*Translator's note: The "Brahmo Samaj" was a non-deistic sect in Bengal whose philosophy emphasized the aspect of the Divine beyond all attributes.]

As the good name of the school spread, highly educated and qualified young teachers began to express interest in joining the institution. Among the first to join was Sri Shashi Bhushan Ghosh from the town of Bankura; he was an M.A. degree holder and a mantra-initiated disciple of Mother Sri Sri Sarada Moni Devi.* Although not a Kriya Yoga practitioner like Yogananda and his follower-friends, Shashi Babu was wholly revered and loved by all of them. It seems that Yoganandaji had said, "So what if Shashi Babu isn't a Kriyavan. When we see him close his eyes and sit for meditation, can anyone say that he is less than us in any way?" Meanwhile, the number of students increased daily and the lack of space became a serious problem. It was concluded that the school had to be relocated. After much deliberation, Maharaja Bahadur himself found a solution by opening up an enormous mansion on one of the properties of Kashim Bazar. Although the lack of space was solved, another more horrific problem confronted the ashram-residents. At that time, these parts of Bengal were beset with a malaria epidemic. Both students and teachers of the ashram became bedridden with the disease. Maharaja Bahadur was extremely distressed. As it was usual practice to change patients' location and climate to improve health in those days, the entire school was moved again to another of the Maharaja's palaces, this time to a place called Madhopur, somewhat far from Kashim Bazar. And though this place was comparatively better, the ashram-residents could not still fully recover from the illness. The exasperated Maharaja then took everyone to his resort house called "Jamai Bari," and while there, the Maharaja himself, along with his very able attendants, nursed and brought everyone back to health. And for a while the austere ashram-residents enjoyed a bit of princely leisure as well. At this time, Ananda Mohan Lahiri—the grandson of Yogiraj Sri Sri Shyama Charan Lahiri Mahasaya—joined the faculty of the school. In any case, this respite did not last for very long; signs of malaria began to show in some students again. To end this once and for all, Maharaja Bahadur sent everyone to his immense palace in Ranchi, situated on a seventy-five bigha [approx. 25 acres] sprawling estate in idyllic surroundings. The ashram and everyone in it were moved to Ranchi in July of 1918. After only a short while, all who were ill regained their health at the lovely Ranchi summer home of Maharaja Bahadur—who also was the Governor of Bihar and Orissa.** No one wanted to leave Ranchi now, although it was only supposed to be a healing retreat. The compassionate and virtuous Maharaja fulfilled everyone's inner wish and designated the Ranchi estate to be the new place where the school would be established. From then on the school became known as the "Ranchi Brahmacharya Vidyalaya" as its official name.

[*Translator's note: Sri Sri Sarada Moni Devi was the venerated wife of Sri Sri Ramakrishna Paramhansa.]

[*Translator's note: Ranchi is in the province of Bihar.]

On the same year that the school was permanently established in Ranchi, the one who followed Yoganandaji like his shadow—Manomohan—became a B.A. degree graduate. Immediately after that, he was initiated by Yoganandaji into the path of sannyas, and was hereafter known as Swami Satyananda Giri. He then completely dedicated himself to the work of the Brahmacharya Vidyalaya. At this time, two teachers of high standard joined the faculty. One was Bijoy Krishna Dutta of Burdwan, who held an M.Sc. degree and was also a student of Acharya Jagadish Chandra Bose, and the other was Pandit Ramendra Nath Bhattacharya from Bishnupur of the Bankura district. Bijoy Krishna was married; Ramendra Nath was unmarried and celibate. The three swamijis were the heads of the school. Yogananda was head swamiji, Basu Kumar was middle swamiji, and Satyanandaji was young swamiji. It could be said that the entire faculty was basically comprised of young people, whether supervisors or teachers. Yogananda was only twenty-five years of age; the teachers were also of similar age, and everyone called each other with the adjunct "dada."* Excepting the three swamijis, the students also called their teachers with the "dada" adjunct, such as: "Shashi-da, Anandada, Bijoy-da" etc. Of course the Pandit Mahasaya [Ramendra Nath] was not addressed as "Ramen-da"; he was simply called "Pandit Mahasaya." Other than Ananda-da, the teachers were not Kriyavans, but everyone in the school had great respect for each other. Acharya Shastri Mahasaya lived in the ashram itself; he was in charge of spiritual and philosophical education, teaching the Gita and other spiritual and philosophical works. He also initiated certain older students into the path of Kriya Yoga, if they were serious in their interest and fit for the practice. From time to time, Gurudev Sriyukteshvarji would come to the ashram for three or four days at a time. During those days, with Yogananda leading the way, the ashram would be filled with a festive atmosphere. It was more or less certain that Sriyukteshvarji would always be present on the anniversaries of the founding of the school.

[*Translator's note: As has been stated previously, the Bengali adjunct "dada" (or "da" in the short form) literally means "elder brother." However, this is used in addressing boys or men who are not from one's family, as an informal suffix of respect for those who are either similar in age or older (never to those who are significantly younger).]

It has already been mentioned that, in those days, there were only two ashram-based schools in the province of Bengal. Shantiniketan—both in patronage and ideals—was open-minded and operated in modern ways; the Ranchi Brahmacharya Vidyalaya took the ancient "guru-kula" ideals and blended them with modern methods of teaching, creating a new educational system by which they were engaged in trying to create societal reform. The students at the Brahmacharya Vidyalaya had to wear garments colored with a natural yellow dye; hair was kept long; as a bedspread or as body-covering for cold, only a wool blanket was allowed; and the use of mattresses or comforters was forbidden. The diet was lacto-vegetarian. To prevent the students' hair from becoming matted, they were required to apply mustard-oil once a week—on the hair and also on the body. But usually the students could not take care of their hair, particularly the young ones, and because of this many of them also had to suffer from lice in the scalp. About this, a funny statement made at that time by an eminent Bengali lady comes to mind. This cultured lady was very interested in enrolling her son in a residential school of excellence and she had been gathering information about Shantiniketan and the Brahmacharya Vidyalaya. Confused about where to enroll her son, she described both schools to her girlfriend and said, "If I enroll him in Shantiniketan, he'll come back with some girl for a wife, and if I enroll him in Ranchi, he'll come back with a head full of lice!" This statement brought to surface an unsaid division that existed between the two schools' environments.

Among the three swamijis, Acharya Yogananda was an open-hearted vessel of love; his deeply spiritual nature and innocent, childlike behavior was attractive and enchanting to everyone. Swami Satyananda was like Yogananda's reflection, and even if he was not the same as Yogananda, he was very dear to the students. Dhirananda was somber, discipline-oriented and a stern enforcer of rules. Sometime later, Swami Satyananda was posted as the head of the brahmacharya vidyalaya in Swami Sriyukteshvar Giri Maharaj's ashram in Puri, and he had to leave the Ranchi school. The scene that was made when he was saying his goodbyes was such that Sriyukteshvarji later jokingly remarked to Satyanandaji, "By the way they kicked you out—it looks like it'll be quite a problem for you to go back to Ranchi!!" But Satyanandaji did not stay in Puri for long; he did have to return to Ranchi. Satyanandaji later said, "The time I spent with my Gurudev in Puri in those days was the greatest time in my life of sadhana."

Journey to America

The year 1920 was the year of greatest transformative importance in Yogananda's life, where the events themselves transpired in somewhat supernatural ways. One Sunday—the off day at the ashram-school—Yoganandaji was lying on his bed, resting in his quarters after the midday meal. The afternoon moved into its later stages. The students were busy playing sports and such outside. Yoganandaji got up and went to the storage room of the ashram, where Bijoy-da—in charge of supervising the meals at the ashram—and the two cooks were organizing and gathering the foodstuffs necessary to prepare the evening meal. Standing in the doorway of the storage room, Yogananda asked Bijoy-da about what was being prepared for the evening meal. But before Bijoy-da could answer, Swamiji became transfixed, looking outside the opposite window, and seconds after that he said excitedly, "Bijoy-da, I'm going to America. I saw just now that I am lecturing in front of hundreds and hundreds of white men and women." And immediately after saying this, he quickly headed back to his room. Bijoy-da and the cooks were shocked and stupefied at Swamiji's exclamation. The Ranchi train station was fairly close to the ashram and the train to Calcutta left a little before dusk. Bijoy-da saw that Yogananda was packing to leave for Calcutta. Within a short time, the students at play found out that their beloved "head swamiji" was leaving for Calcutta in order to go to America. Students and teachers crowded at Swamiji's door; they watched him with pained hearts as he prepared for the journey to Calcutta. As Yoganandaji walked to the station with Swami Dhiranandaji, all of the ashram's residents—basically leaving the ashram empty—followed him, overcome with sorrow. Saying farewell to the one so dear to all the students was unbearably painful for them. Many began to cry helplessly. The teachers were also full of tears, stunned and dumfounded upon hearing from Bijoy-da about what caused this sudden departure to take place out of the blue.

After arriving in Calcutta, Yoganandaji immediately went to his father, touched his feet and presented him with this news that he is going to America. Bhagabati Charan knew his spiritually mad and spontaneous son all too well. Once his son set his mind on going to America, Bhagabati Charan was well aware that that decision was impossible to change. So he asked, "Where will you get the money?" His sannyasi son responded with perfect certainty, "God will provide it." Yogananda's father became silent. Completely swept away with the dream of going to America, Yogananda was all-consumed with finding a way to make it happen. After talking to his old classmates, professors, friends and well-wishers, he found out that there was an international conference of religions being held in the American city of Boston that very year, with representatives from all of the religions of the world. And very quickly, papers to be present at that conference as a representative for India were arranged and procured. What was left now was the financial means for travel. Yoganandaji just could not find it anywhere. During one of these days his father asked, "So! Did your god get any money for you?" Although hurt by this question, Bhagabati Charan's son replied with the answer he had given before, albeit a bit more soberly than before, "God will surely provide it." The father answered, "Let's see which god gets you money!" Bewildered, Yogananda just kept going everywhere round and round, as if he forgot about everything else. Since the time of the vision at the storage room of the Brahmacharya Vidyalaya, it seemed that he became oblivious to all but what the vision foretold. It was so much so that he even forgot to see the most revered and dearest one in his life—his beloved guru Sriyukteshvarji—who had actually prepared him from behind the scenes, step by step, for this very journey. But the ever-compassionate guru kept abreast of every movement of his dear disciple. In any case, the money for travel was nowhere to be found. Yoganandaji's father asked for the final time, "So! Did your god get you the money?" Yogananda's mental state was desperate at the time. Still, he gathered mental strength and said, although very softly, "God will surely give." By that time, Bhagabati Charan's hand had slipped under his pillow, from where he pulled out a piece of paper and handed it to his son, saying, "Here. Take it." It was a bank check written out for a large amount. Yogananda was overcome with tears of gratitude, reverence and devotion as he embraced his father's feet and said, "I know it was God Himself who gave me this money through your hands." With the finances secured, the preparatory matters for the journey to America were completed. Now all of his friends, relatives and acquaintances began to look for the ship schedules and fares and such, and an America-bound ship that would soon be leaving from Calcutta itself was found right away. That ship had only one first class cabin, and it was still vacant. For the sake of time and convenience, that cabin was booked. All of the shopping was done as quickly as possible. No one came to think about the meals on the ship; there was just one person who brought a tin of ghee for Swamiji, thinking that he would need it because he was vegetarian and this ghee could come in handy [because of the possibility of a limited choice of food].

There was only a little time left before the ship pulled away from the port. It had turned at the jetty; all of the passengers were on board; and Yogananda still had no idea how big a task lay ahead of him. Suddenly he saw that his Gurudev was walking with steady gait to the jetty, and upon arriving there, began walking up the steps to board the ship. Feeling both beset with regret and thrilled with overflowing joy, as soon as Gurudev set his foot on board, Yogananda tearfully fell at his feet. The reason for regret: forgetting the ever-compassionate one who prepared him for this path all along, and at the very time of the fulfillment of his loving preparation—the remorse over this was tearing apart Yogananda's heart. The reason for joy: even if Yogananda forgot, his infinitely compassionate guru certainly did not forget to come to bless and encourage his dear disciple on the day of his victorious journey! Sriyukteshvarji picked up his repentant disciple and embraced him, and they both entered the cabin together. What was discussed within between guru and disciple was not possible for anyone else to know. It has been heard that Sriyukteshvarji had a copy of the book he had written—"The Holy Science"—in his hand. After the meeting of guru and disciple behind the closed doors of the cabin, Sriyukteshvarji came out, directly alighted from the ship, and without speaking or looking at anyone present there, walked away from the jetty, boarded the waiting car of Roy Bahadur Atul Chandra Choudhury and departed. When Gurudev was leaving the ship, the previously mentioned book was no longer in his hand; it is possible that he gave it to his disciple on board. Whether before or after deciding to go to America, whether Gurudev's advice was outwardly taken on not, there was never any rift between guru and disciple in their loving relationship. Sriyukteshvarji was aware of every single movement and feeling of the ecstatically inclined and unworldly "child of humanity." The America-bound ship slowly left India's shore and began to move mid-river on the Ganges, carrying Yoganandaji towards the ocean. Although Yoganandaji himself did not know about it, Sriyukteshvarji knew all about the journey to America and news of all of the details of his movements and doings would come to him. With the help of his disciple Atul Babu, Sriyukteshvarji had procured the necessary papers that would allow him to board the ship ahead of time. Roy Bahadur Atul Chandra Choudhury was a respected stevedore at the Calcutta port; therefore it was an easy matter to get the permission papers to board the ship as a non-passenger.

Fellow Passengers on the Ship and First Lecture in English

The only Indian passenger on the ship was Swami Yogananda, and on top of that, he was also the only First Class passenger. Dressed in the flowing saffron colored garb of Hindu sannyasis, long haired and long bearded, he certainly stood out. The other passengers were mostly white Europeans and quite a few were English-Indians—"anglo-Indians." It seemed that most of the other passengers took care to avoid Yoganandaji. He realized that it must be the long hair or the long beard that the passengers did not like. Many of his friends and relatives had commented to him before his journey, "You're going abroad. You should cut your hair and shave your mustache and beard." But he did not pay any attention to these statements. After all he was a sannyasi, and he would go looking like a sannyasi; he was firm on this. Seeing the behavior of the passengers, he may have thought that perhaps he would face the same kind of attitude in America. When the ship anchored at the port of Eden, Yogananda wrote a letter to his friends that he had shaved his beard and mustache while docked at that port. It is possible that the fellow passengers on board were pleased at this, because, other than a particularly rude couple, everyone else began to behave normally towards him. They became especially interested in conversing with him upon discovering that he would be representing India at an international conference of religious representatives from around the world. However, the previously mentioned couple did not hesitate to show their disdain for Yoganandaji whenever their paths crossed. They were full of the racial vanity that was unfortunately typical of many anglo-Indians. Yoganandaji laughed silently within and looked for a way to teach this racially vain couple a lesson. The most tiresome of things to endure on the long liner journeys in those days was the choice of food available to the passengers. Practically every night they were served some sort of dish made of beans, which everyone grew to abhor after a while. Thinking about this predicament, Yogananda found a way to give that couple a taste of his medicine. He spoke to the ship's steward and arranged to make a meal of "luchi" [Bengali deep-fried flat bread] and "aloor dom" [special Bengali potato curry] using that previously mentioned tin of ghee that he had with him. Yoganandaji was an expert cook; this was one of his specialties. The ship's chef agreed to prepare the meal according to his instructions. Meanwhile, Yoganandaji himself invited all of the passengers on board to have this feast of "luchi and aloor dom"—except, very intentionally, that very special couple. As the cooking began, the passengers began to smell the delicious aroma wafting from the kitchen and were overjoyed that they did not have to eat that same bean dish again. The fragrance was mouth-watering to the couple as well, yet they were not invited! The woman of the couple kept walking past Yoganandaji, back and forth, trying to get him to notice. But Swamiji behaved as if they did not even exist. The closer the time of dinner approached, the more the couple became restless. Finally, leaving aside her pride, the lady asked Swamiji, "The aroma of the meal is so wonderful. Won't you please invite us to the dinner?" Seeing a sort of desperation in her eyes, Swamiji laughed within himself and said, "Of course, of course! Both of you are also invited. Of course you will eat with us." Yoganandaji later said that from that day on that couple completely shed their racial arrogance and rude attitude, and behaved towards Swamiji with great openness and camaraderie for the remaining days on the ship. It was during this dinner that Yoganandaji gave the first English lecture of his life. He was not particularly known as a studious person in school, and he had never had the opportunity to lecture in English; nevertheless, he certainly did not lack in courage to carry out his talk. Regarding this first lecture Swamiji had said, "When I stood up to speak, everything got all confused inside my head, and for an instant I even became a bit fearful. I closed my eyes and remembered Gurudev. A good while passed in this silence. I seemed to even hear some smatterings of derision coming from the group! Suddenly I said 'Jai Guru!' [glory to guru] and forced myself to open my mouth. I don't remember for how long I spoke. It seemed like I was speaking effortlessly and fluently—as if it was coming out automatically from within. When I finished speaking and took my seat, a roar of applause went up. Everyone kept saying that the talk was very powerful and profound." Yoganandaji enjoyed the remaining days of the journey on the ship, getting to know and becoming friends with the passengers on the ship.

The Beginnings of Propagation in America

After arriving in America, Yoganandaji went to the conference of world religions in Boston. He was highly praised for his lecture by prominent attendees there. The most noteworthy among them as far as Yoganandaji's work was the eminent and wealthy Dr. Lewis, who was also a citizen of Boston. It was he who began the first Yogoda Satsanga in Boston. He was initiated by Yoganandaji into the practice of Kriya Yoga as well. From this time on, this affluent, generous and dedicated being's love, devotion and reverence towards Yoganandaji remained unbroken. Dr. Lewis was supportive of all of Yoganandaji's endeavors, giving enthusiasm and aiding him in his work. Yoganandaji worked to spread the message of yoga to Americans in many cities, but he could not quite get established in America. He adhered to the renunciate mentality of the sannyasis in order to remain detached from the American way of life. He was not able to earn enough to meet his basic needs. For almost two years, his father had to send him two hundred fifty rupees a month from India.

The Brahmacharya Vidyalaya in the Absence of Yogananda

After writing about Yoganandaji's voyage to America, it is not out of place here to speak about the state of affairs on this side of the world at the Ranchi Brahmacharya Vidyalaya—Yogananda's "first creation"; in fact, this situation which was taking place concurrently needs to also be addressed. As was expected and logical, Swami Dhirananda took over the principal position of the school, and his colleague Swami Satyananda had to return from the Puri ashram. Dhirananda worked his post within the same protocol set by Yogananda, carrying out the responsibilities with perfect precision. Physically impressive, magnetic, virtuous, somber, a strict disciplinarian and an acute observer and enforcer of rules, Dhirananda was not only respected by the students but was feared by them as well. This was because he did not know how to forgive; errors had to be punished. This extremely stern side of Dhirananda's character stood out in everyone's eyes. However, Swami Yogananda and Swami Satyananda were of a completely different character. Love was the most prominent aspect of their nature. The writer has heard this from Satyanandaji: before any of them had become sannyasis, Mukunda had deep affection for Basu Kumar, almost as if he was entranced. But even Mukunda would be taken aback by the sternness of Basu Kumar's character and would comment, "My Manomohan is the one who is good. You are much too 'dry'!" In any case, with Dhirananda heading the school and Maharaja Manindra Chandra Nandi providing financial support, the Brahmacharya Vidyalaya's operations went on smoothly, and the number of students continued to grow. New renunciation-minded, well-educated and righteously-directed students and teachers joined the institution. Particularly noteworthy among them was Kshitish Chandra Basu from Tutpara of the town of Khulna, located in what is known today as Bangla Desh. Handsome, intellectually sharp and eloquent in speech, Kshitish Chandra was regarded with great respect by everyone within a very short time. Because of the continuously growing number of students and the daily increase of applications for new students, Maharaja Bahadur donated another palace for the school's use. This was a two-floor mansion located about four or five miles away from the ashram-school in an area called "Madhuban" in the Chota Nagpur area, on route to the Maharaja's home in Rantu. The palace was situated on a forty-bigha [approx. 10 acres] expanse. This new "Madhuban" ashram was set up for students of the primary grades. The Yogiraj's grandson Ananda Mohan Lahiri was the first head of school for this branch of the Ranchi Brahmacharya Vidyalaya. "Madhuban" was designated for teaching and housing students of primary levels, and the main school was for the students of the upper grades. The daily affairs of the branches were carried out by each branch on its own; however, for special occasions and events, the assemblies took place at the main branch, and all of the faculty and students spent those days together.

CHAPTER 3
Organized Propagation in Full Force

Captain Rashid and Changes in Propagation Methods

For Swami Yogananda, living a life reflecting the austere philosophy of sannyasis—including their non-attached attitude towards money—was not succeeding very well in America. Later, Yogananda would say that lack of success in life had no place in America, and the only accepted and approved mark of success was financial prosperity—being a multimillionaire. And this was the mark of success regardless of the line of endeavor, whether one was a businessperson, worker or spiritual leader. If one was not wealthy, there was no practical way to be established. It was accepted that people should pay to attend conferences; if a conference or lecture was free, then it was assumed that there was nothing worthwhile to be gained from that lecture. There is a practice of ceremonial financial offering at the time of spiritual initiation which is accepted throughout India, that of "guru dakshina" [ceremonial offering to the guru]. In place of the one-time offering of five-rupees as per the injunctions of dakshina in Kriya Yoga initiations, Yoganandaji accepted five American dollars. But if one looked at the financial state of that country, this donation was not enough for the priceless initiation of Kriya Yoga. But Swamiji was not interested in these American ways of doing things; thus, the process of being established was extremely slow; one can even say that the import of the work was negligible. But right when the state of affairs was in this kind of desperate condition, Captain Rashid—Yoganandaji's young friend-disciple whom he had met on the ship during the return journey from Japan—suddenly appeared. Although Captain Rashid was born as an Indian, his behavior and attitude was completely Western. Naturally open-hearted, he had great love for Swami Yogananda. Meeting him after many years, Captain Rashid now came to know about Swamiji's state of affairs in America. After hearing everything thoroughly, Captain Rashid said, "Swamiji! You'll have to forget about the Indian ways of austerity and moving in this snail-like pace. You are in America now; if you want to make roots here, you'll have to master the ways and rules of this country. Otherwise, it would be much better for you to return to India." Swamiji fell deeply into thought upon hearing Rashid's words. He began to think, "It would be quite nice to have Rashid assist me," and other such things. Rashid was not formally employed anywhere at that time. He was a wanderer at heart and spent his time traveling. Somehow provisions took care of themselves. When Swamiji asked Rashid if he would like to help him in his work, Rashid happily said that he would take full responsibility for building the organization. After Captain Rashid joined Yoganandaji in his work, the propagation methods changed completely. He expertly arranged all of the necessities for high-level propagation—renting the best halls in whichever city they would be in, advertising in the most respected newspapers of those cities, putting up posters with color pictures of Swamiji from street corner to street corner, and charging a proper entrance fee for the lectures. Right from the start, Carnegie Hall in New York was rented for a lecture. The rental cost for this hall was high; on top of that, the other preparations mentioned above were also made. The entrance fee was set at one dollar. Rashid had done all of this on his own and then informed Swamiji. Swamiji was shocked when he heard about the arrangements. He said, "Rashid! What have you done? There's not enough money in the bank account to rent Carnegie Hall! If we can't pay the rental fee, we'll have to go to jail!" When Yoganandaji was describing this situation to us, he commented, "It seemed that Rashid believed in the efforts to cause a stir to bring people to Yogoda Satsanga even more than I did. He said, 'Swamiji, what are you saying? If we have to go to jail, then we'll continue with Yogoda Satsanga right from jail itself!'" As it turned out, there was not even space enough for a seed to be squeezed into the hall during the lecture, and Swamiji gave a beautiful talk as well. At the end of it, after all the expenses, they found that they had made a few thousand dollars. The next day, an article came out in a respected newspaper lauding Swamiji and his lecture. Of course, behind this too was Rashid's skillful maneuvering. From this point on, the name of "Yogoda" spread throughout America, and Swami Yogananda was in high demand as lecturer, receiving invitations from many cities and institutions. Money also began to come in abundance, and Yogoda centers were established in several cities. Now arose the necessity of having someone to manage this side of the organization; this was not in Captain Rashid's area of expertise. Thus, word was sent to India for his close friend Dhirananda to come to America. All of Yoganandaji's friends in India knew that Yoganandaji would not keep Dhirananda apart from him for very long. In 1922, turning over all of the responsibilities of running the Brahmacharya Vidyalaya onto Swami Satyananda's hands, Dhirananda left for America.

Founding the Headquarters at Mount Washington in Los Angeles

Swami Yogananda breathed a great sigh of relief after Dhirananda's arrival, as Dhirananda's skill in managing ashram-like institutions was well known. Handing over the entirety of the organizational aspects of the work, Yogananda went on to give lectures throughout the United States. Alongside propagation, there was also tremendous financial gain, and Yogoda Satsanga centers were set up in many cities. Swami Yogananda was now well established in American society. Everyday people looked at him basically as a wealthy man worth hundreds of thousands of dollars. At this time—in 1925—he visited the city of Los Angeles in the state of California, which is situated in the west coast of the United States. This is the city which is also known for the fantasy land of the world of motion pictures—Hollywood. While going about and seeing different sights of the city, one day he went to visit an immense hotel on top of a large hill named Mount Washington. The industrial and crowded cities of America were mostly on the east coast. The western coast of that vast country has rolling hills and mountains linked to mountain ranges such as the Rocky Mountains, which are a bit further inland, running more or less in the same north-south direction as the coast. The eastern part is linked to a mountain range comparatively lower in altitude to the Rockies—the Appalachian Mountains. The areas alongside the Appalachians are known for mines producing coal, iron, copper and other raw materials. One cannot see such huge deposits of so many different types of natural resources located in such close proximity to each other in any other nation. This is why many factories, manufacturing plants and industries related to them were built in this part of the country. Easterners would often visit the west for holidays and health benefiting reasons, especially because there were few industrially dense areas in that part of the country in those days. It was because of this that farsighted businessmen invested in building resorts, hotels and spas in places like Los Angeles and other cities of California. The site that Swamiji went to visit at Mount Washington was also a hotel, established by three friends who had formed a business partnership. Because of conflicts in interest among the partners, the hotel was closed for business and the entire property, including furnishings and land, was ready to be sold to an appropriate buyer. Swamiji had said to us that as soon as he set foot in the building, he immediately knew that that place belonged to him. Finding out that the property was actually for sale, his assistants made arrangements to acquire the sixteen acre property. The enormous hotel was purchased for forty five thousand dollars. At that time, three rupees equaled one dollar, which means that the purchasing price of the property was one hundred thirty five thousand rupees. The entire peak of the mount with the exception of one solitary acre was within the boundaries of this property. Later, even that one acre was acquired and became a part of the center. The magnificent Mount Washington center is thought of as one of three primary sites for tourists in Los Angeles, the other two being the world renowned Hollywood and the city's famous planetarium. The present [1983-84] value of that property is certainly not less than several hundred thousand dollars—quite likely much more. The headquarters of the Self-Realization Fellowship (the name of the Yogoda Satsanga) in America were established at the center in Mount Washington. Yogananda's happiness knew no bounds; with the help of Dhirananda, he had established a permanent structure from where Kriya Yoga could be spread.

Propagation in Different American Cities—Meritorious Recognition by President Coolidge

Leaving the responsibility of running the main center and consequently the work of the branch completely in the hands of Dhirananda—Swami Yogananda went on to travel the whole of the United States, giving lectures, teaching Yogoda classes and establishing new centers. By this time he was renowned in America for being a master speaker. He later said to us that he was counted among the very best lecturers in the country. His compelling voice, beautiful and effortlessly flowing language, and speeches full of spiritual feeling drew listeners in droves, sometimes spilling out of the hall and standing on the street, listening to the talk through loudspeakers mounted outside the hall. Once, in a lecture hall in the southern city of Miami, he had to give talks every day for a week. Overflowing crowds kept packing the hall incessantly. Certain white religious leaders became envious of this phenomenon taking place. With heavily racist tones, they conspired to bring a false accusation against Swamiji and took the case to a court of law. That state had always been infamous for its racism. Swamiji arrived in court on the day of the trial—radiant, magnetically attractive in form, with beautiful yet incisive eyes brimming with virtue. When those eyes cast their gaze on the judge, the magistrate could not withstand its power. "Away with that!"* he said. Regardless of the judge's discomfort, Swamiji was cleared of all charges and walked away in dignity with the highest respect of the court. The next day, most newspapers and journals had their headlines boldly announcing the verdict, and Swamiji's message of practical spirituality went on to gain even more fame. Perhaps nothing exemplified the level of respect that Yoganandaji had attained in America than when the man holding the highest position of all in that country—President Calvin Coolidge—invited him to the presidential mansion [the White House]. Yogananda was the very first Indian to have been honored by an American president in this way. This event was extensively written about in the journals of India as well. When this writer and the one who is presently known as Swami Shuddhananda went to have an audience with Sri Mahendra Nath Gupta, the author of "Sri Sri Ramakrishna Kathamrita" [The Gospel of Sri Ramakrishna], Sri "M" was overjoyed at the news and told us, "Please give Yogananda my heartfelt congratulations." Because of the increase in amount and complexity of the work in America, the need arose to bring more helpers from India. To fulfill this need, former graduate and founder of the students' board of the Brahmacharya Vidyalaya, Sri Jotindra Nath Banerjee—"Jotin-da"—left for America as a "brahmachari" [celibate monk]. At first he was known as "Sri Jotin," possibly following Swami Sriyukteshvarji's precedent of using "Sri" as part of the monastic name. Yogananda restarted this practice in America almost after two decades. Later however, Jotin-da was known by the more usual name of "Brahmachari Jotin" until he was initiated according to scriptural injunctions into the Swami Order by his guru Yoganandaji, after which he was known as Swami Premananda. From that time in 1928 until the present day [1983-84], Swami Premananda has lived in America. He is a man of great accomplishment; one of his greatest achievements has been being the only Asian in the capital city of Washington, D.C. who has an ashram-temple situated on his own personal residential property. There is no possibility any more for anyone to own such a property in that city because the United States Government secured all of the appropriate available land many years ago for the future development of the capital. Like any other capital city in any other nation, Washington is very well known for circulating gossip and controversy. For Swami Premananda to live in a city of this type for this long a period and still maintain the highest level of dignity and respect—much the same as Yoganandaji—up to the very present certainly reflects his great courage and abilities to interact skillfully and graciously with the surrounding society. There were several others besides Swami Premananda who took up the responsibilities of different centers set up by Yoganandaji's mission, such as Sri Nerode in Miami, Sri Ranendra Kumar in Cincinnati and Indianapolis and Sri Khagen in St. Louis. There were many American devotees who were also given responsibilities for running different centers, such as Dr. Lewis in Boston, Dr. Rowan in Cleveland, Alice Gabler in Salt Lake, etc. Yoganandaji and Dhirananda were in the Mount Washington center, and there were several American women devotees who were also there. In some places members of the same family were members in the organization as well, and they basically lived in the center's quarters in a permanent sort of way. One can take for example the Wright family—the mother of the family, two sisters and two brothers. The youngest of the Wright sisters would become Sister Daya and later Daya Mata, the head of the entire Yogoda Satsanga/ Self-Realization Fellowship worldwide. However, many of the participating branches previously mentioned are no longer connected in an official way to the main center.

[*Translator's note: The phrase in quotations is written in English in the original manuscript.]

In order to be able to give the message of Kriya Yoga to large numbers of seekers, Yoganandaji set up a way to spread the teachings through the written medium, which became known as "Precepta Lessons." This method of study and testing can be seen in many universities and other institutes of learning. A very influential American movement known as "Christian Science" gained its popularity and strong foothold in spreading its philosophy by teaching lessons via this very method. To propagate the teachings of Kriya Yoga, Yogananda followed the same procedure set previously by the Christian Scientists. As the philosophy spread to all parts of the globe, the income for the organization also grew immensely, because there was an initial fee to receive the lessons and each lesson also had a separate cost. In 1935, Yogananda said that his Kriya disciples or students in American exceeded one hundred fifty thousand. It is needless to say that this amount of discipleship could have only happened through the above-mentioned lessons in print. In reality, there is reason to doubt whether Kriya can be given or taught properly by letters and circulars. After Yogananda's passing, the Precepta Lessons were increased greatly in number and changes were also made to the original lessons. Yogananda's American disciples of earlier years were not happy with these changes.

George Eastman

It has already been mentioned that Yogananda was thought of as a wealthy man by ordinary Americans. The ashram had around six automobiles, and petrol guzzling cars such as the Pullman could only be afforded by persons of considerable means. And when a person is wealthy, hordes of people show up to follow and praise him. Whenever Yogananda would go to hotels and such places many such people would follow him around. Once he was at a hotel where one of the richest Americans—George Eastman—was also staying. Being the inventor and producer of the Kodak camera, this man of immense fortune was known worldwide. He had quite a few men and women following him around as well. The hangers on from both sides became very excited about introducing their leaders to each other, because getting important persons to meet each other was the usual practice in these types of situations. Swamiji's devotees took him to meet Eastman and both shook hands in greeting. As a gesture of courtesy, Eastman invited Swamiji to see the Kodak laboratories. The offer of such an invitation in itself was the height of civility and graciousness, what to say of receiving it from a man of such great fortune and fame as George Eastman. But Swamiji immediately replied, "Of course! I'm honored to accept your invitation, but on the condition that you first come to see my ashram." At first, Eastman was taken aback a bit; he did not expect Swami Yogananda to attach a condition to the acceptance of his invitation. But because this proposition was made by Swamiji in front of onlookers, he had to accept in order to save face. Swamiji had said that when George Eastman visited Mount Washington, right from the time he alighted from his car, he carried himself throughout his visit with the severity of a man well aware of his wealth and position. At one point he and Swamiji sat on a bench in the garden in front of the mansion. Eastman's behavior was full of the underlying feeling that he was doing Swamiji a favor by gracing the ashram with his presence. They were conversing, but Eastman's responses were serious and very short; there was no expression of any kind of openness. Suddenly, Swamiji looked directly at East-man and spoke out, "Mr. Eastman, do you know that a rich person has no friends?!" Eastman was flabbergasted at this comment. He was leaning regally on the backrest just before this statement; he now started to shrink down into the bench. Then he let go of all of his seriousness and began to talk to Yogananda open-heartedly, laughing and speaking freely, and he spent a long time with Swamiji. George Eastman was an incredibly wealthy man, but he never gave any presents of his Kodak cameras. This time he broke his own rule. After returning home, he sent Swamiji a full set of Kodak photographic equipment as a gift. A short while after this meeting, George Eastman committed suicide, shooting a bullet from his own gun into his mouth. He left a note by his body saying, "Thy task is done. Why wait?"* In his will, he left his vast wealth to be used for charitable work.

[*Translator's note: The quoted statement is in English in the original manuscript.]

Dhirananda Severs with Yogoda Satsanga and Encounters Illness

In the early 1930's, Swami Yogananda's personal life and Yogoda Satsanga's work faced an unimaginable breach. Because of a difference in views, Swami Dhirananda severed all ties with Yogoda Satsanga, and furthermore, cut off all communication and ended all relations with his beloved childhood friend Yogananda. What possibly could have caused a friendship of such strength and depth to break in this way was not known. Thereafter, Dhirananda set out to form another organization to spread the teachings of yoga. There was no questioning his erudition, intellectual brilliance and deftness at accomplishing goals, but perhaps he did not possess the kind of personality needed to attract a congregation, and perhaps he did not have the depth of mystic realization expected of a spiritual leader. Dhirananda sent descriptive letters about his organization to Swamiji Maharaj Sriyukteshvarji and Acharya Shastri Mahasaya in India, seeking their words of support. Sriyukteshvarji did not respond in any way whatsoever. All along, he had disapproved of the extreme closeness with which Yogananda treated Dhirananda. However, Shastri Mahasaya did express his support for Dhirananda's work. From this point on, the two organizations worked separately at spreading the same spiritual message. Dhirananda's leaving left Yogananda deeply hurt, but there was nothing that could be done. He rejected all of Yogananda's efforts at reconciliation. Some time before—around 1925-26—the two friends had planted some fruit trees on the Mount Washington property. One mango tree among them was now bearing fruit. Seeing the mangoes as they were becoming ripe broke Yogananda's heart. They had planted the trees together; one of them was now bearing fruit; how could he possibly eat these mangoes without sharing them with Dhirananda? Yogananda had said that Dhirananda was so proud that in no way could he be persuaded to ever set foot again in the Yogoda center. Religious leaders and associations now invited both institutions for their events. At that time, once Yogananda was invited to a certain church. He was certain that Dhirananda would also be invited. Before leaving for the occasion, Swamiji took one ripe mango and hid it in his pocket. When he arrived at the gathering, he saw that he had surmised correctly; Dhirananda was also there. However, their seats were quite a distance apart. And it seemed that Dhirananda did not want any eye contact to be made between them. Failing to get his attention, Yogananda seized an opportune moment and went and sat next to Dhirananda. He leaned over and said, "Dhirananda, the mango tree we planted is now bearing fruit! I've brought one for you!" Without even looking at Yogananda, Dhirananda said disdainfully, "I have no time for you!"* This rejection struck Yogananda unfathomably deep; the pain was such that everything seemed be enveloped in darkness. And upon receiving this profound blow to the core of his being, Yogananda began to be gravely concerned about Dhirananda's well being. He thought to himself, "Oh no! What terrible misfortune will come upon him now?" He had known from the past the types of repercussions that could befall those who did him wrong. He began to fear that Dhirananda may have to suffer some devastating consequence. When Yogananda was the head of the Ranchi Brahmacharya Vidyalaya, he had seen an example of this type of ramification, just a short while before he left for America. A brahmachari residential student named Dhiren was once looking at a picture of the Lord Sri Sri Lahiri Mahasaya and, for whatever reason, made some unflattering comment about the Yogiraj's physical form. Yoganandaji was nearby. He became overcome with anger and the wrathful words "Your face will become twisted!" spewed forth from his mouth. Immediately, the boy's face, head and neck turned to a crippled and twisted position. Because of this the boy eventually had to leave the ashram. This writer had not yet enrolled in the school. Some of the students who were present at the time are still alive today. The boy's home was on Bechu Chatterjee Street. During 1934-35, when the Calcutta Yogoda Satsanga center and its students' quarters—managed by the students' committee at the time—were on 84 Bechu Chatterjee Street, this poor man came to visit this writer several times. Neck and face twisted to one side, a handkerchief stuffed in his mouth to stop the uncontrollable drooling, Dhiren could barely walk without swaying and his speech was slurred, having difficulty forming words correctly with a crooked mouth. The purpose of his visits was to find out when Swami Yogananda would return from America; Dhiren wanted to fall at his feet and beg forgiveness. When Swamiji had returned, one day at his father's house on Ram Mohan Roy Street, Dhiren turned up. This writer was present at the house at the time. Swamiji was getting ready to leave for someplace or other. He was taken aback upon seeing Dhiren, but did not recognize him. This writer introduced the cursed fellow and refreshed Swamiji's memory about the past incident. By this time, Dhiren had touched Swamiji's feet. Yoganandaji looked at him with deep compassion, but there was no change in the man's condition. Swamiji did not have the power to take back the curse which had sprung forth spontaneously from his heart. Although nothing immediately happened to Dhirananda after his harsh rejection of Yogananda, he fell very ill only a few days afterwards. So serious was the infirmity that he had to be hospitalized. It took about three months of hospital stay for him to recover. But this stay in the hospital profoundly changed the course of Dhirananda's life. The tender, selfless and ceaseless care of a nurse at the hospital helped him regain his health. He fell in love with this kind-hearted woman. Subsequently, he reassumed his family-given name of Basu Kumar Bagchi and left the path of sannyas. The bond of affection and love that had blossomed between Mukunda Lal and Basu Kumar from the beginnings of their youth and which continued later as Yogananda and Dhirananda—a relationship that seemed inseparable—now had no possibility of reunion or reconciliation. Although this friendship was not one that his Gurudev had looked upon favorably, this love had held Yogananda's heart all these years. But the curtain had now fallen on that act in the drama.

[*Translator's note: The quoted statement is in English in the original manuscript.]

CHAPTER 4
Changes; Return to India

Mr. Lynn—Brought by a Supernatural Event

One of the primary qualities of leadership is the ability to draw people; this was certainly evident in Yogananda from his very childhood. His loving nature and dynamic personality were attractive to many people. But keeping the congregation together and on the same track, the organizational skills necessary to manage daily affairs and still expand—these abilities were not within his grasp. Dhirananda and Satyananda were the ones who fulfilled that lack. Leaving Satyananda to run the Ranchi Brahmacharya Vidyalaya and having Dhirananda at his side in America, the propagation of the mission was moving along quite well and easily. Now Dhirananda was gone and the entire responsibility of running the headquarters of the institution was left in Yogananda's inexperienced hands. Naturally the result was problematic. He was never fully abreast of the income and expenses of the ashram, neither could this be expected of him. With unshakeable faith in God and the lineage of masters, brimming with divine spiritual consciousness, carrying out the propagation of Kriya Yoga and witnessing its massive success, Yogananda remained totally absorbed in the beautiful way his life was playing out. One afternoon, he was about to leave the ashram grounds to go somewhere in the city. His car was ready outside. Right at that time, one of the secretaries came downstairs and presented him with a notice from the electric company. The letter said that the ashram still had one thousand dollars outstanding and if this amount was not fully paid by the final due date given on the notice, the electricity would be completely shut off. And the secretary said that the worse part of it all was that there was practically nothing left in the bank. Swamiji was heavily distressed. Known as one of the wealthy men of America and reputed for establishing Yogoda Satsanga throughout the country, finding himself in this desperate financial predicament was certainly a very worrisome thing. He immediately sent the car back to the garage, and instead took the House Car and speedily drove away until he reached an area of the desert about fifteen miles from the ashram. It has already been mentioned that Los

Angeles is rich in natural splendor. Situated by the ocean, Los Angeles also has deep forests, hot and dry desert areas, as well as mountains in the same area of land. It is as if God beautifully decorated this city on every side and placed it on the Earth. Reaching the desert and parking the car on the side of the highway, Swamiji began to walk on the desert sand. He went quite a distance and then sat down in asana right on the sand, and began to cry out his deepest concerns and pains to the Mother of the Universe. When he was describing this later, he said that he kept saying, "O Mother of the Universe! I'm just a sannyasi, I did not ask for fame or fortune—nothing at all! Why give me all of this and then have the pressure of financial want thrown upon me?!" Swamiji did not remember for how long he continued to bring out all of his grief in this way. The desert was desolate and night was growing deep. Completely immersed in his wailing, suddenly he heard someone far away saying, "Ma bhaih! Ma bhaih!" All of his anguish instantly vanished upon hearing this sacred chant. Swamiji felt that this was a sign that the Divine Mother had heard his aching call and was giving him assurance that all will be well. He got up off of the desert floor, walked back to the highway where he had left the House Car and drove straight back to Mount Washington. Swamiji went directly to his room, without speaking or looking at anyone in the ashram, and locked his door. At quite another place, an extraordinary and related event took place that night; that will be brought to light shortly. A few days after Swamiji's prayers in the desert, the ashram received a check for a large sum from an unknown person, accompanied by a message saying that he would like to visit the ashram on a certain day. The donation relieved the organization's financial woes for the time being. Yoganandaji knew that this unexpected gift was a demonstration by the lineage of the masters and the Mother of the Universe, but he told no one about this understanding and kept it completely to himself as he secretly and silently bowed in gratitude for this blessed gift from the Divine. This unknown benefactor's name was Mr. Lynn. On the specified date of his arrival, Swamiji told everyone that if some person by the name of Mr. Lynn should come, he should be taken directly to the prayer chapel of the ashram. Swamiji himself was in the chapel, seated in asana and meditating. Mr. Lynn arrived and was taken to see Swamiji in the prayer house. Swamiji later said, "Immediately upon Lynn setting foot in the prayer house, I saw the entire room of the chapel filled with a blue light. I gave him Kriya right away, at that time!" After he entered the chapel Lynn was struck by seeing the form of Sri Sri Lahiri Mahasaya on the altar and he said in astonishment, "This is the very same saint that came to me in a dream and asked me to send a donation to the ashram!" Lynn went on to describe the dream. The same night when Yoganandaji went to the desert to pray, he had had this dream where he saw an Indian sage asking him to send some financial help to Swami Yogananda. Because of some difference in views, Lynn was at that time living separately from his wife. He was an internationally reputed businessman and possessor of immense wealth and property. Although he had absolutely no lack in material abundance, he was suffering at the time from marital problems. And then came this dream. Lynn did not especially believe nor was he much interested in religion. But he had plenty of money for charity, and he decided to send a donation to Swami Yogananda and see what it would be like to meet him. This supernatural event of the dream is the hidden chapter behind the story of the ashram receiving an unexpected financial donation and the donor wishing to visit the Mount Washington center. Yoganandaji gave Kriya Yoga initiation according to traditional injunctions to Lynn there at this first meeting. Immediately upon the completion of the initiation, Lynn went into a deep meditative trance and remained unmoving in asana for over an hour. From this day on, Mr. Lynn would come to the ashram almost daily, and when he would come, he would go straight to the prayer house and become absorbed in Kriya Yoga and meditation. Often no one knew when he left for home. Because he was a man of such wealth and at the same time so deeply devoted to the practice of Kriya Yoga, the regular presence of Mr. Lynn changed the atmosphere of the ashram. The respect and love for Swamiji deepened. The void that was left in Yogananda's life after Dhirananda's departure was filled for the most part by the appearance of Lynn. The propagation work in America again moved forward with even greater ease.

Directing and Managing the Brahmacharya Vidyalaya—Swami Satyananda

After Swami Dhirananda left for America, the Ranchi Brahmacharya Vidyalaya underwent different advancements under the direction of Swami Satyananda. Swami Yogananda was a dreamer type of being; forgetting about Ranchi or seeing Ranchi as being lesser in priority while consumed by new circumstances in America was not a surprising thing. The hope was that Dhirananda would keep Yogananda aware of the operations and events in Ranchi. But that was for naught. Instead, it was heard that Dhirananda was completely uninterested in Ranchi matters and he felt that whatever was going on in the Brahmacharya Vidyalaya was of not much importance at all. On this side, the young Swami Satyananda—the youngest of the previous triumvirate—continued to direct the Ranchi school as he best saw fit with co-workers of the same age or slightly older than him. He regularly sent word to his spiritual brother and leader Yogananda, keeping him abreast of the goings on in Ranchi. When Swami Satyananda took on the mantle of director, all of India was alive with a nationalist consciousness. Led by Mahatma Gandhi, India in 1921 was astir countrywide with the independence movement through non-violent civil resistance. If other ideologies or cultural and societal activities did not follow the same line, they were either not given much weight, or looked at in an unfavorable light. The Ranchi Vidyalaya also was not free from this atmosphere. The freedom movement consisted primarily of well-schooled youths, and the teachers and students of the Brahmacharya Vidyalaya were all highly educated young men; it was only natural that the nationwide uprising would stir them as well. In any case, the monthly financial support from Maharaja Manindra Chandra Nandi continued unabatedly, and the number of students continued to increase. The school now had a reputation throughout the land for not only upholding and teaching the ancient ideals of India, but also for moving progressively with the ideas of independence and national self-reliance that had now gripped the nation. At this time—among several others—two scholarly young teachers joined the school, Ashwini Kumar Datta and Shishir Kumar Raha. Both had completed their college studies and taken up Gandhiji's motto of non-violent civil resistance. Following the initial uprisings, they became fully involved in spreading the message of national freedom. It has to be admitted that because of many such young people joining the school, the fundamental philosophy of the Ranchi Brahmacharya Vidyalaya went through some changes. The founder and his assistants had dedicated their lives to the path of Sri Sri Lahiri Mahasaya's Kriya Yoga. Now, although the school was still spiritually oriented, other ideologies, such as nationalism, also found important places in the collective mentality of the school. However, Lahiri Baba's path was still held in the highest position, above all else, and the practice of celebrations at certain astrologically significant times of the year—according to the precedent set by Swamiji Maharaj Sriyukteshvarji—went on regularly. But the students no longer had an ideological unity as before. Of course, it must be understood that the high ideals of civil resistance would take hold more easily in the tender minds of young people. Here are some examples of the differences within the faculty: Shashi-da—Shashi Bhushan Ghosh—was a mantra-initiated disciple of Sri Sri Mata Sarada Moni [wife of Sri Sri Ramakrishna Paramhansa]; Kshitish-da—Kshitish Chandra Basu—was a disciple of the great Vaishnav guru Sri Sri Radharaman Charan Das Babaji; Ashwini Kumar was a disciple of Sri Sri Swami Bholananda Maharaj of Hardwar; and Shishir Kumar was a disciple of the Videha Mahanta Sri Sri Santa Das Babaji. These devotees of these different luminary saints also held Sri Sri Lahiri Baba in the highest regard. Although this open spiritual environment benefited the students, the possibility of an atmosphere of conflict was also present. The person whom Satyanandaji relied upon to help prevent a disruptive situation was Ananda-da, Yogiraj's grandson Ananda Mohan Lahiri. However, the real power—financial power—was still under Satyanandaji's control, at least as long as financial support continued to come from Maharaja Manindra Chandra Nandi. And this aid gradually became less and less, as part of the management of the affairs of his properties came under the control of a holding company. Subsequently this control had to be turned over to the governmental Court of Wards. The previous flow of revenue and expenditures resulting from doing business as a private landowner inevitably came under greater restrictions now that the proprietorship was in the government's hands. Funds for the various charitable institutions and works liberally provided by the Maharaja were significantly curtailed. These budget restrictions also eventually affected the Brahmacharya Vidyalaya, leading to a lessening of the monthly aid that the school received. After the passing of the magnanimous Maharaja Manin-dra Chandra Nandi in 1929, even this aid came to an end. The author at that time had completed his studies at the Vidyalaya and was beginning his college years. How far the financial restrictions had gone can easily be seen by examining the money allotted for the Maharaja's funeral in comparison to other events of similar importance in the past. The Maharaja's grandson's annaprasan [Hindu christening] cost four hundred thousand rupees; that same valiantly generous Maharaja's funeral was allotted only fifty thousand rupees. It is heard that the Queen Mother took another fifty thousand out of her own depository to somehow be able to carry out the funeral. The Brahmacharya Vidyalaya was invited to the memorial service, and along with Swami Satyanandaji, the author and Pari-mal Kanti, another graduate of the school, were also present at Kashim Bazar. Although solemn, the royal service seemed quite lavish to the writer and his friend, but the older dignitaries present knew the splendor with which events such as these were held in the past, and seeing what they considered to be tightfisted arrangements, they commented that the Maharaja himself should have kept aside and specified a proper amount to be spent for his own funeral. From this event, one can see the financial condition the Maharaja's estate was in at that time. Raising funds for the Brahmacharya Vidyalaya became a matter of great concern. Still, regardless of many problems, the school continued to "hold its course," mainly because of Swami Satyananda's cool head and enterprising mind. Somehow the ideals of Lahiri Mahasaya were kept alive at this yogic educational institution and the members of the faculty did not have to take up an alternative philosophy in order to continue. However, the nationalistic atmosphere gripping the nation was quite present at the school. Kshitish Chandra Basu—Kshitishda—was appointed to the position of president/director for the Ranchi branch of the Congress party, and he eventually became a member of the "Gandhi Seva Sangha," the organization which was set up and supported by an icon of renunciation and public service—a man who was known as "Manabhuma Gandhi"—Sri Nibaran Chandra Dasgupta of Puruliya. In the words of Netaji Subhas Chandra Bose, the Gandhi Seva Sangha was the "iron foundry" for those carrying out Gandhiji's message. Thereafter, to direct the Brahmacharya Vidyalaya more along the lines of these new open-minded ways and nationalism, a new, parallel institution was founded, called "Brahmacharya Sangha." The Ranchi Vidyalaya became the central school of the sangha [association]. Satyanandaji was appointed as this sangha's first president. He had no choice but to accept this position, although he maintained that he did not want to give up financial control of the school. At the time of this conflicted situation, the members of the Ranchi Brahmacharya Vidyalaya's Graduated Students' Committee—founded by Jotin-da, or Brahmachari Jotin, later known as Swami Premananda—were the only ones on Swami Satyananda's side, determined to keep total control of the school's finances in Satyanandaji's hands. After Brahmachari Jotin left for America, the responsibilities of managing the operations of this committee were turned over primarily to Sailesh Mohan and this writer. It seems appropriate here to write about some of the methodology by which the school was run. Familiarity with these procedures and practices will shed light on how the ideals and goals of the institution were realized.

The meals served at the school were completely vegetarian [lacto-vegetarian]. On certain astrologically significant days of the month, arrangements were made for the food restrictions specified for those days. Milk and sometimes ghee were served during the main meals at midday and evening. Each student had a plate, bowl and drinking glass, which each was responsible for cleaning and maintaining. Besides the main meals, light repasts were taken twice a day, which the students themselves served. The students also attended to seeing guests, taking care of those who may be ill, seeing to the needs of the teachers and other such usual duties of the ashram. One of the five heads of the Students' Committee—appointed by the committee itself—acted as director as well as liaison between the faculty, the heads of school and the students. The times for carrying out the various duties of the day and night were made known by the ringing of a bell. Once a week, the director of the committee announced the names of specific persons who would be appointed to carry out the essential duties during the week, including the name of the bell ringer. Historically, the school had a policy of emphasizing a respectful attitude toward those who were assigned the weekly tasks and discouraging the students from forming exclusive groups; this was partially accomplished by selecting the appointees for the week by secret and anonymous voting. It is quite amazing to realize how open and unbiased the students were. The bell-ringing duty was a very important one. The ringer's job was to strike the bell exactly in line with the hands of the clock at specified times, signaling the beginning of a period in which to carry out some necessary activity of the day or evening. If a person did not discipline himself to have a keen sense of time, giving him such a job would not only be useless but a detriment to the workflow of the ashram. The ringing of the bell announced all of the various parts of the entire program of the day, from pre-dawn brahmamuhurta [time of God]—when it rang to awaken the residents and get them out of bed—till the time to go to sleep at night. In any year, this duty was only entrusted to two or three select students and not given to others. There were also specific ways of ringing the bell. If the bell was heard distinctly as one stroke, and then another stroke and so on—one stroke at a time—that was a signal for: 1) arising at brahmamuhurta, 2) the time of respite or the ending of class during the time of day when class was held, or 3) the time to go to bed after the evening meal.* If the bell was struck with two strokes close together—two at a time and then two more and so on—that signaled everyone to gather at the prayer house after dawn or after dusk for daily prayers. If there were three strokes at a time—three and then three more and so on—that announced the beginning of class; classes were held outdoors under trees in the garden of the school, each class under a separate tree. Hearing four strokes at a time was nectarous to the students' ears as that signaled the meals, any of the two main ones or the two light repasts. Five quick strokes at a time announced the time of body and hair oiling and the subsequent time of bathing. Before the time of bathing as well as after finishing homework in each student's respective rooms, eight strokes grouped together and repeated told everyone that it was the time for working on different crafts and practical skills. Skills such as weaving, sewing, bookbinding, first aid, simple horticulture etc. were taught by certain teachers with expertise in these various areas. After the time of bathing, the bell was struck with nine strokes at a time, telling everyone to gather at the prayer room, this time for the fervent recitation of sacred verses in song form. If the allotted work was not accomplished up to this point, then the bell was not rung for the four-stroke signal that was to come next and was kept silent, and that signal was for the announcement of the midday meal. Thus it can be seen that the carrying out of the entire program of the day depended upon the orderly ringing of the bell. There was a special signal of three separate strokes which was a call for everyone to gather in front of the prayer house, no matter what the activity one may be engaged in at the time. This was usually a sign that a special announcement was to be given to everyone by the head of school himself. This happened usually during summertime, particularly during bright fortnights, sometime close to the time of the full moon. The head of school would announce an outing for the students to some serene place in the hills or some nearby forest; often a picnic of some sort was held. When Yoganandaji was the president of the school, this practice was more or less a regular one. It was basically the same during Satyanandaji's time as well. The wonderful memories of those days still bring back the joys and thrills of youth even for those former students who have now passed into their twilight years.

[*Translator's note: It is usual practice in India to eat the evening meal right before retiring for the night.]

There were age limits set for enrollment as residential students at the ashram-school. Students could only enter the residential program if they were between eight and twelve years of age. Applications for entrance below or above these limits were rejected. It was under Satyanandaji's directorship that exceptions were made regarding this strict rule. The rule was first broken for what seemed to be a singular reason, but afterwards the restrictions were overlooked many other times. There was an interesting event behind this as well. Satyendra Nath Mukherjee of the town of Howrah was a residential student of Shantiniketan [Rabindranath Tagore's school]; he was past the age of twelve. At that time, Shantiniketan's head of school was an Englishman by the name of Pearson who was very fond of Satyendra Nath. The boy loved religious practices but there was no environment for that at Shantiniketan. Pearson kept himself fully abreast of the different establishments in India advocating traditional Indian culture. After thinking about it deeply, he decided that it would be good for Satyendra Nath to enroll in the Ranchi Brahmacharya Vidyalaya. Satyendra Nath no longer had his mother and father; he had only an elder brother for a guardian, and he was also quite young. Thus, the possibility of Satyendra Nath's elder brother going against this proposition could not arise at all, particularly when a man of such high scholarly status as Mr. Pearson suggested it. Pearson himself took the initiative and wrote to the head of school of the Brahmacharya Vidyalaya, asking permission for Satyendra Nath to be enrolled as a residential student in Ranchi. Because the boy was past the age of twelve, Satyanandaji cordially wrote that because of age restrictions, he regretfully could not accept Satyendra Nath as a student. The letter that Pearson wrote in return, upon receiving the note of rejection, was the reason that this strict age-limit rule was first broken. Satyanandaji told us, "Mr. Pearson opened my eyes. He said, 'Children are like the softest clay. Whatever container they are put in determines the shape they will take. It is not at all right to reject a student just because he is slightly older than the age limit allows.'" Satyendra Nath was thus accepted, although somewhat as an experiment. Mr. Pearson himself came with the boy to enroll him and stayed on as a guest of the school for a few days. And Satyendra Nath truly did turn out to be an ideal student of the Brahmacharya Vidyalaya. Although he was not particularly good at studies, when it came to conducting worship services, tending to the ill, serving elders and other such service-oriented activities, he carried these out perfectly, in line with the highest standards of the ashram. On top of this, his respect for all people, especially elders, and his cheerful and lighthearted nature won over everyone's hearts. In due time, Satyendra Nath was initiated into the path of Kriya Yoga by Acharya Shastri Mahasaya, and later, he formally took the vows of a "brahmachari" [celibate renunciate] with the rites performed by Hardwar's Mahatma Swami Bholananda Giri, after which he was known as "Brahmachari Satyananda." Just before Bholananda Maharaj left his body, he bestowed on his primary disciple Swami Mahadevananda the title of "head of temple." Following Bholanandaji's directions and conducting the ceremony in his very presence, Swami Mahadevananda initiated Brahmachari Satyananda into the path of sannyas, giving him the name of Swami Sanakananda Giri. Sanakananda was the first sannyas initiate of Swami Mahadevananda after Mahadevanandaji became the head of temple of Bholanandaji's sannyas-ashram, and according to precedence, Sanakanandaji had the right to succeed Mahadevanandaji for the seat of the temple head. But Sanakanandaji did not stay long at the Hardwar ashram. In the city of Oudh [Ayodhya], a matted-haired sage left the sum of one hundred thousand rupees in Sanakanandaji's name before he left this life. Sanakanandaji took this gift and built an expansive institution dedicated to social service. Ever drawn to treat the infirm, Swami Sanakanandaji was a certificated homeopathic doctor, and was well known in that region [Ayodhya] particularly for his treatments of eye-problems. Everyone referred to him as "Doctor Maharaj." His personality was also very influential in this part of Uttar Pradesh [name of province], so much so that he was nominated to run as a parliamentary representative for the Ayodhya area against a member of the powerful Congress Party. Sanakanandaji lost to the Congress Party member by only a few votes. Around 1978-79 he left this mortal plane. He traveled to many parts of Europe, Afghanistan and other countries, leaving a legacy of reverence and respect—seen by many as their guru—and being known throughout as one who exemplified spiritual richness. Satyendra Nath's model life set a high standard indeed for students at the Brahmacharya Vidyalaya to reach for many years to come. Swami Satyanandaji was successful in his experiment when he overlooked the age-limit rule regarding Satyendra Nath; he later relaxed these reins several times and was successful in those cases as well. This writer himself was able to study as a residential student at the Brahmacharya Vidyalaya because of Satyanandaji's loose interpretation of this regulation.

The Brahmacharya Vidyalaya after the Maharaja's Passing

It has been stated in the previous section that Maharaja Manindra Chandra Nandi, the primary financial supporter of the Vidyalaya, passed away in 1929, and that after his passing, the support from the Kashim Bazar estate grew leaner and leaner until it ultimately stopped. The worsening of the estate's financial solvency began to be evident towards the end of the Maharaja's life. In order to resolve these fiscal problems, the management of the estate was handed over to an English firm by the name of Guilenders, but in the end all business affairs of the estate were assumed by the Court of Wards of the government. At this time, the Maharaja came to Ranchi for a health respite. He rented an immense mansion by Bariatu Hill, quite a distance away from the ashram. One day, this writer accompanied Satyanandaji on a visit to see the Maharaja at that rented house. It was strange to see this king who owned two palatial mansion-estates in Ranchi having to rent a house for his retreat. It was as if he had become like the "babui" bird [the weaver bird having to weave yet another nest]. Ironically, both of his mansions in Ranchi were being used by the Brahmacharya Vidyalaya. In conversation, the Maharaja expressed his perturbation at the Guilenders firm and said that in the name of improving the financial condition of the estate, they were trying to find a way to shut down the Brahmacharya Vidyalaya and stop the programs of village education supported by the Maharaja. How much the Maharaja loved and respected the Brahmacharya Vidyalaya can be seen by his actions at this time. Renting this place regardless of owning the palaces used by the Vidyalaya, he even invited all of the residents of the ashram for a massive midday meal at his rented retreat. Everyone, from the little "brahmachari" children to the scholarly teachers and administrators, came for the feast. The time had moved well into the second part of the day, but because brahmacharis [saintly ascetics] had not yet been fed, everyone at the house had maintained a full fast—without even water—until that point [a Hindu custom]. When Swami Satyanandaji was made aware of this, he asked the Maharaja to please not continue with this kind of suffering. The Maharaja's son, Prince Nandi, was standing right next to his father. The king poked his son's belly with his right index finger and said, "I don't have a problem with this. Look at him. He seems to have plenty in his stomach!" The tall, powerfully built and handsome prince was a bit embarrassed by his father's humorous remark. Everyone laughed. The Maharaja himself stood there and directed the servants until the child "brahmacharis" had finished eating, and towards the end he even began to serve the ashram-students by his own hand. Everyone was amazed at the venerable king's devotion and reverence to those who were far below his age and social status. Quickly, the Maharaja's son-in-law more or less forcefully snatched the pot of sweets from his father-in-law and took over the role of serving everyone the last part of the meal. This event demonstrated the true nature of the valiantly magnanimous Maharaja Manindra Chandra Nandi's heart.

Another financially related matter—the founding of the Brahmacharya Sangha and making the Brahmacharya Vidyalaya as its center—has also been previously mentioned. During this association's tenure, a branch of the Brahmacharya Vidyalaya was established in an area by Rikhiya, near Deoghar, under the benefaction of the eminent public leader and attorney Kumar Krishna Datta Mahasaya, on a large open area in Koshama, which was part of Datta Mahasaya's expansive estate. The author's brother-like friend Sri Panchkori De was appointed to head this branch. A short while afterwards, Swami Satyanandaji was stricken with a severe heart ailment and stayed in a house in Rikhiya for rest and recovery. The year was 1933. In any case, Satyanandaji returned to Ranchi after some time, and Panchkori De came back as well, closing up the branch in Koshama.

Sri Panchkori De Disciple of Shastri Mahasaya (Kebalananda)
and brother-like friend to Sri Dasgupta ji

Yogananda's Return Journey to India

The episode of Yogananda meeting Mr. Lynn has been previously described. That meeting happened around 1932. The beginning of this wonderful relationship seemed to be a preparatory precursor to Yoganandaji's return to India. It was as if the scene was set for everything to go well under the patronage of Mr. Lynn. On the other side, it was important for several reasons for Yoganandaji to return to India, not the least of which was his first major "creation by will"—the Ranchi Brahmacharya Vidyalaya. The preconceived return became reality in 1935. One day, Yoganandaji was in a superconscious state and heard the call of his Gurudev asking Swamiji to come to him, indicating that the great master's time to leave the mortal frame was at hand, and if Yogananda did not come as soon as possible, there would never again be another chance to see each other physically. Swamiji was overcome with restlessness and wanted to run to his Gurudev. But the funds to travel to India were not available at the time. Nevertheless, Swamiji had completely made up his mind that he will make the trip back to India without a scintilla of doubt. The ashram-residents close to him became concerned. How will the travel expenses be met? When word of this got to Mr. Lynn, he immediately took it upon his own shoulders to meet any costs necessary for Yoganandaji's trip. He also suggested that Swamiji should see

some other parts of the world by automobile during his travel before finally
setting foot on his motherland. In 1935, there were a total of three Ford
Tourist motor cars that were available for sale; one of those very cars was
purchased for Swamiji. And Mr. Lynn provided Swamiji the money for all of
the costs—those of taking that car on a ship across the world and on trains
in those parts of the world, automobile maintenance, petrol costs, insurance,
and the expenses of Swamiji and his two assistants traveling with him. Thus
Swamiji's return trip to home was arranged to be in royal fashion.

On this side in India, before word of Yoganandaji's return was even
received, an incredible event related to his coming back took place in Ranchi.
Swami Satyanandaji was in Ranchi at the time. In the temple room of the
prayer cottage, there was a Shiva lingam, an enormous picture of Yogiraj
Lahiri Baba hanging on the wall, and a full-body picture of Yoganandaji—
drawn by Sananda Lal—on an easel. There was another door to that temple
room, located on the side of the No. 4 Ward. During the hot summer, the
residents would sometimes keep that door open to let in a cool breeze. One
night, a student from that ward suddenly woke up from sleep and saw through
that door that Swami Yogananda's radiant form seemed to be coming out
of that picture in the temple room. The student became frightened when
he saw this supernatural scene. In the morning he told Satyanandaji of the
event. Swamiji did not say anything at all to the student at that time, but
he later told this writer, "When I heard about that incident, I knew that the
'boss' was definitely coming this time. I've seen these types of things happen
around him [Yogananda] at other times, since we were children!" Just a few
days after this event, a letter from Yoganandaji arrived in Calcutta, saying
that he had begun his journey back to India.

Forming a Welcoming Committee for a City-wide Reception in Calcutta

After fifteen long years of residing in distant America, Yoganandaji's return in
the sixteenth year as the pride of Mother India naturally caused a nationwide
stir. And there was no end to the expectant excitement and joy felt by those
friends, relatives, students and disciples who had been blessed to have had
his company, as well as the graduated and presently enrolled students of the
Brahmacharya Vidyalaya who had held Yoganandaji in their hearts as their
ideal role model although they had never seen him. Not only were they
excited about seeing him in person, but a new hope had arisen that his arrival
would bring on a new and torrential current of progress at the Brahmacharya
Vidyalaya and Yogoda Satsanga. At that time, other than the Brahmacharya

Vidyalaya, the only centers whose work was related to the practice of the Kriya Yoga of Lahiri Mahasaya were a students' association and residence run by graduates of the ashram-school and the Yogoda Satsanga of Calcutta. Thus, the responsibility of the best possible welcoming preparations for Yoganandaji fell on this association and the Yogoda center as a matter of course. The chairman of the students' association and residence at the time was Sri Ramendra Nath Das. Ramen-da and co-presidents Sailesh Mohan Majumdar* and Sailendra Bejoy Dasgupta (this writer) were the administrators. Looking after residential matters was Sailendra Bejoy's responsibility. Sudhir Chandra Roy—Sudhir-da—regularly stayed in the students' quarters. Immediately upon receiving news of Swamiji's return, an urgent meeting to assemble a welcoming committee was called by the association. Many of the graduates of the Vidyalaya were present at this meeting. Sri Bishnu Charan Ghosh was especially asked to attend. Although Bishnu Charan was not an official graduate of the Brahmacharya Vidyalaya, the right to make this demand of him was nevertheless proper. When Maharaja Manindra Chandra Nandi had first visited Yoganandaji's tiny shack of an ashram in the slums of Calcutta, Bishnu Charan was there, dressed as a child-brahmachari to welcome the Maharaja. But the main reason for asking him to come was because he was Yoganandaji's youngest brother and he was known in the exclusive circles of Calcutta. The weight of responsibility to form the welcoming committee was put on Bishnu Charan, and, along with him, on this author. Bishnu Charan's task was to gain the support of the dignitaries of the city and put together a welcoming committee of set members, and this writer's work was to go to Bishnu Charan's house— morning and evening, hurry him out of the house and then go together in his car to meet the elite and distinguished people of Calcutta. Among those in the assembled welcoming committee were: the successor Maharaja Nandi of Kashim Bazar, Santosh's maharaja Manmath Nath Roy Choudhury, Mr. Bijoy Pramad Singharoy, Mr. Hari Shankar Pal, Lt. Col. Mr. Hassan Suravardi, the former mayor of the Calcutta Corporation and public leader Santosh Kumar Basu, and several other such eminent citizens. Santosh Kumar Basu was appointed president of the committee. It was arranged that when Yoganandaji arrived, he would be garlanded on behalf of the citizens of Calcutta by the then mayor of the Calcutta Corporation—and the future Sher-e-Bangla—Maulavi Fazlul Haq.

[*Note: Sailesh Mohan Majumdar later became Swami Shuddhananda Giri.]

On the Way Back to India with His Companions and Traveling in Different Countries

Accompanying Yoganandaji on his return journey to India were Charles Richard Wright—the brother of the one who is presently known as Daya Mata—and Miss Ettie Bletch, who was a sister [female devotee] at the Mount Washington center. Wright was a young man who was capable of driving an automobile and who served as Swamiji's personal secretary. Ettie Bletch was middle aged and was Swamiji's attendant. The three of them traveled in the new automobile from the west coast of the United States to the east coast metropolis of New York and boarded a ship headed for London. The car was put aboard the ship. On the way to New York, another person joined them for the overseas journey, a young man who was the son of Dr. Lewis, the wealthy patron and follower from Boston whose support had been so essential during the early days in America. After arriving in London, Wright had the car released from the ship, and that car took Swamiji to many places of attraction in England and Scotland. The English newspapers had announced his presence in Britain. There were many transplanted Indians as well as British men and women who were lovers of Indian philosophy and spirituality, and they wanted to at least see Yoganandaji with their own eyes and possibly hear him give a talk. Lectures were set up in many places. Most of these were managed and conducted by Kedar Nath Dasgupta, the founder of the Vishva Dharma Sammelan, who also introduced Swamiji to the audiences at the lectures. The biggest of the talks took place in Caxton Hall in London. The attendance was so large at this immense hall that there was no room to even stand. Swamiji's profound and powerful lecture, filled with energy and spiritual wisdom, captivated the hearts of everyone there. He went to Scotland by car as well, particularly because of a personal invitation by the distinguished citizen Sir Harry Lowder. After spending a few days on Scottish lands, Yoganandaji and his fellow travelers crossed the English Channel from the port of Dover in England to the port of Calais in France. Of course, the car was with them. From here they traveled by that automobile to many parts of Europe, such as France, Germany, Italy, Belgium, Holland, Switzerland etc. Hitler had begun to rise in Germany at that time and the entire country was being molded to a new set of uniformity and rules. The scenes in that land at that time brought up feelings of great admiration in Yoganandaji. He used to say that the entire German nation was alive, and that it was absolutely mesmerizing to see groups of young men marching together with the "clack, clack" sounds of their boots resonating in unison. Little did he know that this so-called "beautifully arranged garden" would be obliterated to dust within a decade and fall into the horrific annals of history. The most significant part of the travel in Germany was seeing the world-renowned, God-intoxicated female saint Theresa Neumann. This great woman was distinguished by an unbelievable miracle that occurred to her regularly. From her very birth, signs of wounds appeared on her body in the same places where Lord Jesus Christ bore the nails driven into His hands on the cross. These wounds in Theresa Neumann's hands would become red on every Friday, and sometimes even bleed on their own. It was an annual miraculous event on every Good Friday, when her wounds from her hands would drip blood. Hundreds of thousands of Christians from around the world came to see her every year and felt blessed to have been in her presence. The day that Swamiji went to see her was a Friday. All of her wounds were bleeding. Swamiji said that Richard Wright was with him at the scene; Sister Etta and Dr. Lewis' son were elsewhere. Wright fainted and fell to the ground upon seeing Theresa Neumann's bleeding wounds. After this, Yoganandaji and his companions traveled to Greece, Asia Minor, Jerusalem and Egypt, and eventually boarded an India-bound ship at Port Sayed. It was here that Swamiji was forced to ask Dr. Lewis' son to return to the United States because of the young man's ill health. The three travelers now were booked along with the car for Bombay. It was from this place that news came to Calcutta that Swamiji would be arriving in Bombay very soon and that he had two persons accompanying him; one of them was a man who acted as his personal secretary and the other was a middle-aged woman who was his attendant and who cooked his meals and such things. This writer remembers that when he received this news and took the letter to Swamiji Maharaj Sriyukteshvarji and read it to him, Swamiji Maharaj sat up in his easy chair and asked, "Who did you say are coming with him?" When he heard that one of the two people accompanying Yoganandaji was his personal secretary who also drove his car and the other was a woman who tended to his cooking and such, Sriyukteshvarji sighed and sank down in his easy chair in a somewhat disappointed way. After a short silence, he again sat up and said, "Look, I need to see him on a personal level. I thought that because Yogananda spent all these years in the West, perhaps he may have acquired a habit of drinking tea. Seeing him after all these years, it's only right that I offer him and his companions some tea." Saying this, Sriyukteshvarji clapped his hands and called a child brahmachari to come. He asked the boy to open the nearby closet and bring a sack that Swamiji Maharaj had brought from New Market. Sounding a bit serious, Swamiji Maharaj said, "I thought that if I should offer him tea it would be proper to serve it in a silver cup and saucer. Now if I serve Yogananda in a silver cup, I must do the same for the other two as well. For this reason, I went to New Market two days ago and brought three sets of silver cups, saucers and spoons. Now I hear that one of them is a driver and the other is a cook!" And then he seemed to become extremely disappointed by this and again sank back into his chair. It did not matter how much this writer tried to make him understand that these two people were Yoganandaji's disciples, that they did these types of jobs as they are necessary. Being an elder and experienced, Gurudev did not want to hear any of this. He just kept on muttering, "One—a driver, and the other—a cook!" It was impossible to reason with him at that time with any kind of logic. As it was, the best logic in this case was to just keep quiet.

Arrival in India

Yoganandaji and his companions arrived in Bombay and headed for Calcutta by train. However, he temporarily deviated from his destination, breaking the journey at the Wardha station and taking his assistants to see Mahatma Gandhi's ashram in Wardha. Among the many matters discussed in a heartfelt conversation with Mahatmaji, subjects such as Kriya Yoga and diet were also brought up. Gandhiji was devoted to the practice of "ahimsa" [non-violence or non-aggression]; he was vegetarian and did not even eat eggs. Swamiji suggested that for the sake of health, one could consider eating unfertilized eggs because there were no sentient lives being taken. Gandhiji listened to Swamiji's words intently, but he did not make any comment on this matter. Yoganandaji and his assistants eventually left Gandhiji's ashram and took the next Calcutta Mail [name of train] from the Wardha station and again resumed their journey to Calcutta.

Most likely, Swamiji set foot in Bombay on September 16, 1935. Either on that very day or perhaps the next day, the respected English-language newspaper in Calcutta, the Statesman, printed an essay written by Yoganandaji himself. The essay was titled "India Replies." In 1929, an American woman had written a book called "Mother India," in which she had said many derogatory things about India and her culture. This essay was composed as an answer to the insulting remarks in that book. At that time, Swamiji was in his main organizational center at Mount Washington. One day, a gentleman arrived at the ashram with the aforementioned book and handed it to him, saying, "Swamiji, here. Here is the picture of your India." Swamiji was lying down on his belly and resting at the time. There were a few American devotees around him. Right after looking through the book, he began to write. Wright said that he completed the entire essay at one stretch from that resting place. From a general perspective, the article was quite well written and the erudite language made it a pleasure to read. In certain places a critical finger was pointed towards the dark sides of American life which were scrutinized sternly. The purpose of this essay was to show that no culture was perfect in every aspect. Just as a country which is spiritually developed may have ordinary folk who are spiritually unaware—like India, the same can be true for a land that claims to be superior in the empirical sciences—like America—and its ordinary citizens may be equally unaware of basic scientific facts. This should not be a cause for countries to insult each other. Instead, it should bring different cultures together so that they may be able to help each other. No doubt, the article was written to bring about intelligent discussion. And it was only natural that uncovering and exposing the seamy side of American life would be thought of by Indians, especially young people, as an appropriate answer to Miss Mayo's derisive remarks about India's downtrodden cultural condition. One of the duties this author had at that time was to inform Guru Maharaj about the goings on with Yoganandaji after his arrival. So, on the way to see Sriyukteshvarji to tell him about Swamiji's arrival in Bombay, this writer took that newspaper article with him with the intention of showing Gurudev how his spiritual son was leading the way in inspiring feelings of love for India in the hearts of many. A few days before this time, Sriyukteshvarji had become disappointed regarding Yoganandaji's companions; so this writer thought that perhaps this essay would cheer him up. The writer reached Serampore, went to Sriguru's house and gave him the happy news of his dear disciple setting foot on his motherland. Sriyukteshvarji was certainly very pleased to hear this although he did not show any particular outward emotion. Then the writer spoke about the Statesman article that had greatly moved the hearts of the youths of Calcutta, and that the article had added to the atmosphere of high-spiritedness and reverence around Yoganandaji. The writer unfolded the paper and showed the article to the Master. Sriyukteshvarji said, "Why don't you read it to me? Let's hear what he's written!" The writer happily began to read. When a section came up about events that frequently took place in the deep night in a certain part of New York City, Swamiji Maharaj said, "Read it to me again, will you—what he's written." The writer now began to feel a little trepidatious inside. Upon hearing that section read to him once more, Swamiji Maharaj stared at the writer with a strange and questioning look and asked, "You're saying that Yogananda wrote all this?" Responding with an affirmative, the writer defended the article and put forth that Yoganandaji did not write anything like the derogatory remarks that Miss Mayo had printed in her book against India; instead, he had given a very appropriate reply to her insults and did so as civilly as possible. Sriyukteshvarji had no time to hear this kind of reasoning. Again, he had only one thing to say, "You're saying that Yogananda wrote all this? Shame, shame!" Saying this, he listlessly sank back into his easy chair again. The writer was shocked at witnessing this reaction—absolutely dumbfounded. It would take some time to comprehend such a response regarding the spiritual leader of India's young people by his infinitely wise and knowledgeable guru himself. Sriyukteshvarji certainly had the right to know how his spiritual son was carrying out the mission for which he was sent overseas, a mission which the Master took so much care to make possible: the mission of spreading, teaching and initiating people into that which was known as India's greatest treasure—the science of awakening spiritual awareness. Guruji could not imagine that Yoganandaji would be interested in keeping informed about the sordid activities of American culture. After all, Yoganandaji was a messenger of India's spiritual teachings, the symbol of spiritual life! Having had his efforts to give Swamiji Maharaj good news soundly rejected a second time had the writer kicking himself again and again.

Welcome Arrival in Calcutta

It was the 18th of September, 1935, the day the Bombay Mail [train] was scheduled to arrive at the Howrah Station. A sizeable crowd had gathered at the plat-form—many devotees, Indians interested in the higher life, people from all walks of life. Everyone from the Calcutta Yogoda center, as well as Sailesh Mohan and this writer, were there with garlands and bouquets in hand. If memory is served correctly, the writer recalls that he and Sailesh Mohan came to the station in Bishnu Charan's family car. Bishnu Charan went separately to bring the Rolls Royce automobile belonging to the Maharaja of Santosh, Sir Manmath Roy Choudhury, because it was previously decided that Swamiji should be taken to his family home in that vehicle. The Bombay Mail came to Calcutta through Nagpur, and from Nagpur to Calcutta it ran on the Bengal Nagpur Railway [line]. It was sarcastically said by many that the acronym of the Bengal Nagpur Railway—"B.N.R."—stood for "Be Never Regular," because the trains on this line were notorious for being chronically late. But Swamiji's train came more or less on time. It was a matter of great luck that the first class car in which Swamiji was riding stopped exactly in front of this writer. Swamiji was already standing at the door of the compartment. As soon as he set foot on the platform, the writer hailed "Guru Maharaj Ki Jai!!" [Glory to Guru, the Great King!!], touched Swamiji's feet and garlanded him as the throng resounded "Guru Maharaj Ki Jai!!" in answer. Swamiji was surrounded by everyone in joyous celebration and taken to the waiting Rolls Royce nearby. Others were also getting ready to board their own means of transportation to journey back to Calcutta-proper. Right at this time, Sailesh-da—Sailesh Mohan—whispered, "Look,

I know 'Bishtu' [Bishnu Charan] and his people; they will forget us and leave without us. I've brought money. Come, let's hire a taxi and go with Swamiji's car." So it was in a taxi that Sailesh Mohan, the writer and a couple of others followed Swamiji's car and eventually arrived at Swamiji's father's newly purchased house on Ram Mohan Roy Road. It would not at all be an exaggeration to say that the reception at home—by father, brothers, sisters-in-law, nephews, nieces, other relatives and friends—was well beyond even the likes of which could be normally expected when any triumphant child of the family returns home after many years. Elder sister Roma Devi's welcome was especially stunning. She was there to receive her spiritually heroic younger brother with a ceremonial bouquet of flowers; her eyes were meditatively serene. As soon as she came in front of him, she fell at his feet with the bouquet still in her hands. Swamiji, completely unprepared and shocked by this act, cried out, "Bada-didi [elder sister]!! What are you doing?!!" But by that time, the elder sister had already accomplished what she set out to do. Swamiji spent the first part of the day in that festive atmosphere, reuniting with relatives and friends. And the writer's full-time duties with him began from the second half of that day onward.

The next day, meaning the second day after Swamiji's arrival in Calcutta, the writer went to see him in the morning. As he entered, Swamiji looked at Richard Wright, who was also in the room, and said, "Look, look! Does he look just like Mahadev Desai or what?" During the short time that Swamiji was at Mahatma Gandhiji's sevashram [ashram of service] in Wardha, he had become friends with Gandhiji's sole secretary, the eminent Mahadev Desai. Perhaps in Swamiji's eyes something in the writer's appearance and behavior looked similar to Desai's. However, the writer himself could not find any likeness other than both wearing plain white cotton clothes. It was on that very day that Swamiji let everyone know that the writer was his sole Indian secretary, and Richard Wright was his sole American secretary. The writer felt very blessed to have been given this unimaginably fortunate opportunity for service. Whenever and for as long as Swamiji stayed in Calcutta during his more than one year in India, the writer was graced to be in Yoganandaji's constant company. However, the writer was not with him when he traveled the northern and southern parts of India.

As far as one can remember, it seems that it was on that second day after arrival in Calcutta that Swamiji went to Serampore in the car brought from America to have darshan [holy visitation] of Sriguru. The writer did not accompany him there. Thus he was not able to witness the wonderful reunion of guru and disciple. In any case, Gurudev was relieved of his "tea serving concerns" because it turned out that Yoganandaji did not drink tea. A brief description of this reunion can be found in Wright's account of it in the March 1937 issue of Inner Culture magazine.

Reception by the Citizens of Calcutta

The next significant event was a formal public reception held by the citizens of Calcutta. As previously mentioned, the credit for putting together the welcoming committee belonged solely to Bishnu Charan; the writer was there only as his assistant. This reception took place just a few days after Swamiji's arrival. The exact date does not come to mind. At that time in Calcutta, there were only three proper venues for holding this type of a public event: Town Hall, next to the Calcutta High Court; Albert Hall on College Street; and Ram Mohan Library Hall—the smallest of the three. Town Hall was the largest, but because it was at the edge of the city there was an issue with travel, which would mean that there would be less of a crowd. Albert Hall was in the center of the city with easy access. The main room of the venue was also of quite a respectable size. The place where the "Coffee House" of College Street stands today, drawing students during their leisure time, was where Albert Hall once stood. The venue was completely full with an audience eager to see and hear Swamiji. Most of the members of the welcome committee were present along with other distinguished citizens. The Maharaja of Santosh, Manmath Roy Choudhury, adorned the presidential seat; next to him on two sides were Maharaja Sachindra Nandi and the former mayor, Santosh Kumar Basu. It was Santosh Basu who performed the customary recitation of an honorary letter of felicitation on behalf of the citizens. He then presented the letter as a gift to Swamiji. The president of the committee and all of the members present honored Swamiji with similar graciousness. Yoganandaji was the main and final speaker of the occasion. Among the people on stage was elder guru-brother [disciple of same guru] Sri Motilal Mukhopadhyay. Gurudev Sriyukteshvarji was not there. The writer sat on the stage floor, right at Swamiji's feet by his chair. Before the event commenced, Swamiji slightly laughed and asked the writer, "Should I speak in Bengali or English?! Shouldn't I show them how well a Bengali boy learned to speak in English?!!" The writer happily expressed his agreement and said that it would be great to hear him give the lecture in English. And Swamiji did give his lecture in English. Before beginning, he pushed aside the microphone in front of him and began to address the audience directly. With a deeply resonating voice, powerful language and incomparable mannerisms and gestures, his love-filled, spiritually eloquent speech mesmerized the entire crowd. With this incredibly beautiful talk, we were able to catch a glimpse of the magic by which Swamiji had gained the endless praise and admiration of thousands and thousands of men and women in America. He had said that he was thought of as one of the two greatest speakers in America at that time. That was certainly evidenced by this lecture. This welcome reception and Swamiji's talk was highly lauded by the newspapers and journals. Praise spread throughout the city by word of mouth as well, and Swamiji's presence caused a considerable stir in the minds and hearts of the people of Calcutta.

Visiting the Ranchi Brahmacharya Vidyalaya

Now Yoganandaji began to plan for a visit to the very first establishment he founded, the Ranchi Brahmacharya Vidyalaya. News was sent to Ranchi. Meanwhile, at his father's house in Calcutta, there seemed to be some sort of competitiveness going on between his two younger brothers Sananda Lal and Bishnu Charan, both vying for the greatest amount of time and closeness with their illustrious brother. At first, upon seeing Bishnu Charan's bodybuilding center, his accomplished young students of physical culture, as well as his capacity to build an organized institution, Swamiji was duly impressed. However, when it came to the Ranchi trip, it was Sananda Lal who was chosen. Two automobiles were to be taken for the journey, Yoganandaji's Ford Tourist and Sananda Lal's six-cylinder Buick. Richard Wright was the Ford's driver and Sananda Lal himself drove his Buick. Both cars were filled snugly with passengers. The writer and Satyanandaji's younger brother, the late Nalini Mohan Majumdar, rode with Sananda Lal. The cars departed fairly early in the morning with the intention to reach the Vidyalaya in Ranchi by afternoon. But that goal could not be reached. While traveling on Grand Trunk Road, somewhere near Asansol, the Buick began to have mechanical problems and we had to stop. It took some time before the journey could be resumed. However, the passengers experienced no discomfort. Swamiji sat everyone down right in the middle of a field by the side of the road, and he fed and entertained us all with many wonderful stories. In the meantime in Ranchi, Satyanandaji, with his teachers and students, began to look towards the road with expectation as early as noon. The students had beautifully decorated the school and its surroundings with flowers and plants. Some small fireworks were procured for the festivities as well. They were prepared to be set off just as Swamiji arrived. Several of the distinguished citizens of Ranchi also came to the ashram in the afternoon, hoping to give Swamiji a grand welcome. But all had to return to their homes with disappointed hearts. By the time the two cars reached the Vidyalaya it was almost midnight. Tiredness took over many of the waiting students, and they went to sleep on the floor or the ground, wherever they happened to be at the time. Knowing that the ashram-residents may be asleep, the horns of the cars were repeatedly sounded, as a sort of signal, right from the time the ashram property was sighted until the cars entered the grounds. Everyone in the Vidyalaya hurriedly got up, wiped their eyes and got ready to welcome Swamiji. The fireworks were lit and there was a resounding call all around, shouting out to everyone that Swamiji had returned "home" to his ashram. Satyanandaji, upon seeing his guru-like friend after so many years, understandably lost his composure and could not hold back his tears as they embraced each other. Swamiji was given a large room, in which there was one large bed for his use and another bed in the opposite part of the room. Students and teachers who came in to talk with or listen to Swamiji during his stay went to sleep right in that room on the mat on which they sat. The other bed was for Ananda-da—Yogiraj's grandson Ananda Mohan Lahiri—and the writer. In Calcutta, Swamiji had said many times that during the night, it was only his body that slept, he was ever awake. Whispering this statement in the writer's ears, Ananda Mohan—after Swamiji had fallen asleep and begun to snore—said very softly, "Swamiji, we are awake." Immediately Swamiji answered back, "I know all that." We tested him again during that same night, and again he answered back immediately, just like before. Swamiji spent the next morning in the joyful meeting and greeting of the residents of the ashram and many people of distinction that had come to see him. In the afternoon, he took several of us by car to the Bhorenda marketplace near the edge of town. We were walking around and seeing the sights when all of a sudden Yoganandaji noticed an aborigine farmer sitting with a basket full of mushrooms for sale. Swamiji gleefully cried out, "Look! God gives me whatever I wish for. Come, let's take the whole lot!" When the party returned to the ashram, it was the writer who was given the responsibility for cooking those mushrooms, and at dinner, as Swamiji ate the dish prepared, he complimented, "It has been a delicacy."*

[*Translator's note: The quoted statement is in English in the original.]

On the third day at the ashram, Swamiji held and conducted a Yogoda class. The purpose of this class was to inform many people at once about the matters of Kriya Yoga. It was in this manner that Kriya Yoga was spread in the West. Those who were not interested in Kriya Yoga did not attend this class. Among the people who came on the journey from Calcutta, Tulsi-da and Prakash-da—Tulsi Narayan Basu and Prakash Chandra Basu, respectively—did not attend this class, just as they would not when the class would be held in Calcutta, and stayed outside on the veranda. Noteworthy among those present was the eminent geologist, the elderly Pramath Nath Basu, one of Ranchi's most respected citizens, and the eminent scientist who located the prime spot for the Tata firm's ironworks factory. This event was memorable by the demonstration of fixing a student's hand on a wall, so that the person could not pull it off, by pure mental power. The boy was a resident-student of the Vidyalaya, about seventeen or eighteen years of age, and as he had no parents, his sole guardian was his maternal uncle who raised him in the city of Memio in Burma. He was enrolled in the Ranchi Vidyalaya because it provided solid education in a righteous environment. After his talk, Swamiji called this boy and announced that he would now show everyone a demonstration of how powerful the mind actually is. Swamiji said that he would fix this boy's hand on a wall. The boy was taken to a nearby wall and told to hold his arm horizontally on the wall with his palm flat against it. Then Swamiji sort of massaged that arm with his own hands, from the boy's armpit to the palm, and said, "Now the hand is stuck!" Swamiji tried to move the hand and showed that it could not move. The boy also could not move it himself. The readers may remember that, in his childhood, it was in this very same way that Swamiji stuck his household cook's hand to the wall. Until Swamiji himself came and touched the hand and said, "Now the hand is free!" the boy could not free himself, just as the incident with the cook. The writer, who also had been in Burma during childhood, had a conversation with the boy. Probably feeling some affinity with the writer, the boy spoke openly when asked about his experience. He said that he became terribly afraid just seeing Swamiji, as if his life was flying out of him—a strange feeling would come over him. Whenever Swamiji came to the Ranchi ashram after this incident, the boy would do whatever he could to avoid Yogananda. He would run away and sit on a distant field. After spending several days in his old, memory-filled, "first-creation," Swamiji and party boarded their two cars and headed in the direction of Calcutta. On the way, around midday, they stopped to pay respects to a very advanced yogi at his house in Burdwan.

This great yogi was Sri Sri Kumar Nath Mukhopadhyay, known to Bengali readers by his pen-name of "Sudhakar." This sage was famous for his collection of writings, which consisted of unique translations of the great Sanskrit scrip-tures—such as the Gita, Chandi etc.—in the Bengali poetic meter known as "payar cchanda." It is most likely that the only rendition of the verses of the Gita in Bengali payar cchanda is his. As a writer, he was known as "Sudhakar" and the collection of his writings was called "Sudhakar Granthavali" [collection of books by Sudhakar]. In his youth, he became extremely attracted to the path of Lahiri Baba's Kriya Yoga after reading and hearing about it from Acharya Panchanon Bhattacharya's writings and lectures. Kumar Nath wrote to Kashi Baba Sri Sri Lahiri Mahasaya in Benares, asking to be initiated into the practice of Kriya Yoga as established by Him. In response, the Yogiraj wrote back telling him to go and see Acharya Panchanon Bhattacharya in Calcutta. Thus one morning, Kumar Nath took a train to Calcutta. After arriving there, he began to walk in the direction of Bhattacharya Mahasaya's home in Ahiritola. He had to pass through a neighborhood of ill-repute known as "Sonagacchi." As he was going through that area, Kumar Nath's sight fell on the girls standing out in the verandas of the upper floors of the houses. However, he had no lustful intentions in his heart. Suddenly, he saw Bhattacharya Mahasaya pass by him, with upper body bare, draped with a towel for bathing; he was rubbing oil on himself as he walked towards the Ganges to take a bath. Kumar Nath thought that Bhattacharya Mahasaya must have seen him looking at the girls, and he shrunk in shame. Feeling a bit low, he went to Bhattacharya Mahasaya's house anyway and waited on the front porch for him to return from the Ganges. But he waited for good long while and there was no sign of Bhattacharya Mahasaya. It was getting close to noon. Then someone from within the house opened the door and saw Kumar Nath standing there. The man asked him why he was waiting there. He said that he was waiting to see Bhattacharya Mahasaya; he had seen the acharya going to take a bath in the Ganges, but where was he? It had been quite a long time! The man from the house said, "No sir! He hasn't gone anywhere! He's in the house!" Saying so, the man went into the house for a short while, came back and invited Kumar Nath inside. Acharya Mahasaya was sitting in the front room itself. Kumar Nath touched his feet and said, "I saw you going to bathe in the Ganges, but why did I not see you come back?" Acharya-dev answered, "No, I've been sitting here in this same place since morning. I haven't gone anywhere! Oh! You say you saw me? Well, I suppose people see a lot of things." Kumar Nath was astonished. What a way to begin the practice of Kriya Yoga! After staying at Kumar Nath's residence for a few hours—taking pictures of him and his wife, separately and together, as well as pictures of Swamiji and Kumar Nath together—in profound bliss and spiritual intoxication, the party took leave of the great yogi and resumed the journey back to Calcutta. This meeting was the beginning of a collection of material that would later be written in book form by Swamiji—in his "Autobiography of a Yogi"—about the great sages of India.

Obtaining Control of the Property Rights in Ranchi

While he was in Ranchi, Swamiji came to know that the estate of the Maharaja of Kashim Bazar was in terrible financial trouble and that Maharaja Srishachandra Nandi was trying to sell all of the property and assets of the Vidyalaya—the ashram, garden, residential quarters and all—for the sake of financial solvency. So, immediately upon returning to Calcutta, Swamiji had his youngest brother Bishnu Charan set up a meeting with Maharaja Srishachandra. He did not speak about this to anyone but Bishnu Charan. They met on the specified day, and after the customary greetings and precursory small talk, Swamiji brought up the subject of the Vidyalaya and wanted to know if the Maharaja really wanted to sell that property in Ranchi. The Maharaja explained the financial condition of the estate and confirmed that he was eager to sell all of his Ranchi properties. Hearing this, Swamiji responded firmly, "You cannot destroy the glory of Kashim Bazar! So—if you do not take offense at this, and you do not feel that I am being sly in some way—I propose that you turn over the property of the Vidyalaya to me. As far as the financial problems associated with the property on which the Vidyalaya is operated, I will pay its selling price, no questions asked." The property was in the name of the Queen Mother of Kashim Bazar and its price was 30,000 rupees. The Maharaja agreed to the proposition. As part of the exchange, the "Madhuban" palace, which was being used as the branch that handled the primary grades, was returned to the Maharaja. It came to be known that this transaction was possible through the help of Mr. Lynn in America. Later, on the 1st of January in 1937 at the Mount Washington center, Swamiji himself announced that this purchase could be made because of donations by Mr. Lynn and the American devotees. After the ashram-school with its expansive land and gardens was purchased under the name of Yogoda Satsanga, Swamiji made the Ranchi ashram the headquarters of Yogoda Satsanga in India. The teachers of the Vidyalaya who were members of the Brahmacharya Sangha left the ashram on friendly terms, and started the Brahmacharya Vidyalaya anew on Bijoy-da's property in an area known as "Nivaranpur" on the outskirts of Ranchi. However, all of the residential students of the original ashram remained with Yogoda, and the school on the Yogoda property was now renamed "Yogoda Satsanga Brahmacharya Vidyalaya."

Annual Festival at the Calcutta Center

Besides taking care of the property issues concerning Ranchi, the other matter of significance in Calcutta for Yoganandaji was the yearly festival at the Calcutta Yogoda center—the public gathering for the Autmnal Equinox and the feast after it with friends, devotees and followers. The celebration was coordinated by the ever-active duo, co-organizers Saliesh Mohan Majumdar and Sailendra Bejoy Dasgupta. Attendance was huge that year because of Yoganandaji's presence at the celebration. Albert Hall was again chosen for the public address, and Swamiji was the primary speaker once more. Present at the meeting were Gurudev Sriyukteshvarji, Maharaja Srishachandra Nandi and Swami Satyanandaji, along with elder guru-brothers Acharya Motilal Mukhopadhyay, Amulya Santra, Amulya Das, Charu Mitra and other such luminaries. The main attraction was Swami Yogananda's discourse. On this day Swamiji's lecture was in Bengali. This talk was also captivating, just as the previous one in English. It was not possible to surmise that it was his first Bengali lecture to a public audience of this size. Towards the end of the speech, in order to demonstrate the power of mind over the body, he asked the audience members to stand up and clasp their own palms tightly together. Swamiji instructed everyone to intensely think that the hands were now inseparably stuck together and could not be separated. He counted out loud, "one, two, three…" up to six, and then exclaimed that the hands were now joined and could not be separated. It was observed that almost two hundred of the audience members could not pull their hands apart. Then Yoganandaji pulled his own palms apart, saying, "Here! Now they're free!" Almost everyone who had their palms fixed to each other were able to free their hands after seeing him do it, except for seven poor souls whose palms were helplessly stuck together. Yoganandaji called them to the stage and he himself helped six of them unclasp their hands. But the seventh one's palms just would not open. When this person approached the stage, Moti Babu— Motilal Mukhopadhyay—suddenly began to stir restlessly in his chair. This fellow was Moti Babu's disciple, a doctor by profession, known to be miserly, and—as it was found out later—was basically a bundle of nerves.* It turned out that in front of sages and saints this man simply became paralyzed from nervousness. No matter how much Swamiji tried to unclasp the man's palms, the more it seemed that the entire structure of his upper appendages became more stiff and twisted. Finally, Moti Babu stood up and said to Swamiji, "You won't be able to help him. I'll take him." Saying this, Moti Babu took the man outside the hall. The writer was sitting on a low platform right next to Swamiji's feet and was watching everything. When Moti Babu ushered the man outside, the writer followed them. Moti Babu gently caressed the man's back and said, "There now my child. Everything's all right now. It's all right." After about four or five minutes of this, the gentleman finally regained a sense of normalcy and his hands were eventually fine. The writer had also tried to get his palms to become stuck together exactly according to Swamiji's instructions, but nothing happened. Upon returning to Swamiji's residence

after the meeting, the writer asked him, "Swamiji, I was sitting closest to you. Why is it that nothing happened to me?!" Swamiji laughed lightheartedly, looked slyly at the writer and said, "It won't happen to you. You're a critic.**"
A few days after the festival, when the writer went to see Guru Maharaj Sriyukteshvarji in Seram-pore, the very first thing that Maharaj ji said was, "What is this that Yogananda showed? There is nothing spiritual at all in this. These are nothing but tricks.***"

[*Translator's note: The phrase "a bundle of nerves" is in English in the original.]

[** and ***Translator's note: The words "critic" and "tricks" are written in English in the original.]

Swamiji now came to the weekly meetings of the Calcutta Yogoda Satsanga held every Saturday and because of his presence, the gatherings were full of life and profound spiritual feeling. Before the commencement of each service, Swamiji would say that only if there were five or six new attendees would he allow himself to partake of prasad [sacramental food]. The writer knew the count would always be definitely more than that, because every time Swamiji came across anyone he knew, he invited them to the satsang [spiritual meeting], which meant that dinner would also be served for these guests at the ashram. The writer used to prepare for twenty-five or thirty guests, but not only did the numbers exceed this estimate regularly, sometimes more than fifty or sixty people came. If it got to be too late in the evening, the residents of the ashram had to send for food from a restaurant, sometimes a good distance away if nearby places were closed. Whenever Swamiji would see someone he knew, he would say, "Come to our center. It's a beehive of spirituality. You'll find great joy there." And it was absolutely true; as long as he was present, at least once a week that small center became transformed with the atmosphere of a spiritual beehive.

Yogoda Class

At this time, a sort of outdoor lecture hall was created in the garden area on the north side of Swamiji's father's house on Ram Mohan Roy Road. A canopy was hung and fabric was draped on all four sides to form quite an acceptable space for gatherings on the lawn. A platform serving as a stage was set up on the east side of this space, and a chair was situated in the center of the platform. There were benches and chairs placed on the ground in front, facing the stage. It was in this space that Swamiji held his

American-style sessions of giving Kriya Yoga initiation to many people at one time. Only those who were already initiated into the practice of Kriya Yoga or who were going to be initiated were allowed in the sessions. It comes to mind that, during the first such gathering, Swamiji's childhood friend Tulsi Narayan Basu and Swamiji's follower Prakash Das took care to remain outside. Swamiji sat on the chair on the stage and those who were being initiated sat on the chairs or benches facing the stage. After speaking about all of the preliminary and necessary aspects, Swamiji asked the writer to come on stage and demonstrate the techniques of Mahamudra and Kriya Pranayam to the aspirants. Far from telling the writer that this was about to happen, Swamiji did not even give the writer any sort of hint that he would have to show these things in front of people. It must be understood that in traditional practice, Kriya Yoga initiation is given in secret. In any case, Swamiji was happy to see that his instructions were carried out. Then he himself conducted the final and absolutely important part of the initiation, "Jyoti Darshan" [seeing inner Light], showing the technique personally and individually to everyone. Before concluding the session, Swamiji said that the new initiates should regularly visit the Calcutta Yogoda Satsanga center where they could learn everything about the path and spirituality. He said that the center was an "Inner Circle."* Later, the writer asked Yoganandaji, "Swamiji, initiation is a secret affair between guru and disciple, and it is also an event that begins a deeply connected relationship between them. Can a mass initiation produce the same result?" Swamiji looked at the writer from the corners of his eyes and said, "Look, I want to throw the net far and wide, so that at least a couple of big fishes can be caught." The next time the writer met Gurudev Sriyukteshvarji, he described the event of this mass Kriya initiation to the Master. Gurudev sat quietly, listened to all, and then said, "This thing about the 'Inner Circle'—this is beautiful. Tell everyone that there is a lot more to know, and if they come to the 'Inner Circle,' they will get to know everything." Then, regarding Swamiji, Gurudev said, "Let him do his own work. You and the others go and spread well the word of the 'Inner Circle.'"

[*Translator's note: The words "Inner Circle" are written in English in the original.]

CHAPTER 5

[Translator's note: For Chapter 5, there is no heading text below the words, "Chapter 5", unlike the previous four chapters.]

Royal Guest of the Kingdom of Mysore

Kali Puja [worship of Goddess Kali] and Diwali [festival of lights celebrating the beginning of the New Year in many Hindu calendars] were imminent. Captain Rashid, former director of operations for Yoganandaji's work in America, as well as former assistant and lifelong friend, was now an aide-de-camp* of the young king of Mysore [now a province], and he was also the king's dear friend. He knew that Swamiji was in India. The festival of Diwali was a royal affair in the kingdom of Mysore and celebrated with regal pomp and flair every year. Through Rashid's suggestion, Swamiji was invited to be a guest of the kingdom at this event. And an incredible event concerning a lame person took place while he was there as a royal guest. There were some enthusiasts in Bangalore who were aware of Swamiji's supernatural abilities. Many in the city were interested in having Swamiji give a spiritual talk, and a public lecture was arranged to be held in a large hall. Several persons asked Swamiji to demonstrate something supernatural. One of these people found a lame man and brought him to Swamiji. This man had to walk on one leg and on crutches, as the other leg was permanently crippled in a bent position. Swamiji looked directly into the man's eyes and said, "Do you believe I can heal you?" The man answered that he had complete faith that Swamiji could heal him of his lameness. Swamiji later said that the man's eyes showed that he did have complete faith. Swamiji then told his companion to bring the man to the public meeting on the following day. The next day, the lecture hall was full, and no announcement had been made regarding the lame man. After Swamiji took the stage, the crippled man arrived with his companion and made his way to the platform. Swamiji indicated that he wanted to have the man brought up on the stage itself. When the man came on stage, Swamiji went very close to him, looked at him directly into his eyes and again asked, "Do you have complete faith that I can heal your leg?" Swamiji later said that, from all indications in his outward appearance and his behavior, the man seemed to have complete faith in him. Swamiji kept looking at the crippled man and then suddenly kicked away one of his crutches. The man was shocked and about to fall, when Swamiji commanded with tremendous power in his voice, "Stand up!!"** The man looked at Swamiji's eyes and, like a machine, stood straight up on both legs. Then Swamiji commanded again with that same firmness and power, "Walk!!" And, like a machine turned on, the man walked off the stage down to the main floor of the hall. The entire audience was stunned. The walls shook with roaring and endless applause. The following day, the Bangalore Observer and another daily newspaper ran front-page, full-page stories with bold headings, resplendent with commentaries praising this miraculous event.

[*Translator's note: The term "aide-de-camp" is in French [Roman alphabet] in the original.]

[**Translator's note: The quoted statement is in English in the original.]

Traveling in Different Parts of India

After his travels in the province of Mysore, Swamiji went to other parts of India before returning to Calcutta. Among these destinations was the ashram of Sri Ramana Maharshi in Tiruvannamalai. This holy place, a pilgrimage site for the spiritually thirsty, had quite an influence on Swamiji. He was particularly affected by Yogi Ramiah, an adept sadhak-disciple of the Maharshi. When the two of them met, at one appropriate moment they both looked into each other's eyes and became still for quite a while. Swamiji later said, "During that silent exchange as we looked into each other's eyes, I was almost touching the 'Eternal-Boundless.'"* Richard Wright, acutely perceptive and quick, captured this scene forever in his camera. After coming back to Calcutta, Swamiji quietly told this writer, "It seems like that disciple is even more advanced than his guru!" There was one particular thing of note regarding his travels in South India. Swamiji did not go to Pondicherry and did not express any particular interest in wanting to see Sri Aurobindo [sage in Pondicherry].

[*Translator's note: The term "ananta-aseem" or "Eternal-Boundless" is in quotation marks within the quoted statement in the original.]

Organizational Attempts in Calcutta

Immediately after Swamiji returned to Calcutta, Bishnu Charan made every effort to establish himself as Swamiji's closest person, and at the same time tried to help himself with Swamiji's widespread and immense influence. Swamiji was also quite taken by Bishnu Charan's accomplished students of physical culture at his health and fitness center. He began to think that these physically fit youths and their leader Bishnu Charan would be able to bring new life into the work of Yogoda Satsanga in India. Naturally, the enthusiastic workers of the past gradually fell to the rear of Swamiji's attention and focus. An institution needs finances to move forward; there was no shortage of wealthy people in the country; what was needed was only a way to attract them. Bishnu Charan had a millionaire supporter—Sheth* Yugal Kishor Birla of the Birla lineage. Shethji was very much a miser, but when he saw physically fit youths, it pleased him and he helped them. Bishnu Charan used to put on exhibitions of physical fitness, demonstrated by his many students, and receive financial prizes from the Sheth. Birlaji also was very happy about Bishnu Charan's methods of work and aspirations. Seeing that Bishnu Charan had made the discipline of high-level physical culture available for Bengali Hindu youths brought great joy to the Sheth. It was through his help that Bishnu Charan was able to found large centers of physical culture at the Jadavpur College, Benares Hindu University and the Kangri Guru-Kula Ashram in Hardwar. The salaries for teachers and assistant instructors—graduates of Bishnu Charan's school—were also provided by Shethji. There was an astounding feat that Yoganandaji was able to do—stop his heart from beating. And he could also demonstrate this tremendously advanced yogic ability in front of people, and had done so many times in many different public meetings. He had performed this feat publicly in quite a few places in India as well, like the time when he demonstrated it in front of a number of political and royal dignitaries at the Nikhil Bharat Kshatriya conference. Bishnu Charan wanted Swamiji to stop his heart at a gathering of millionaire sheth Marwaris [people of Marwar] and thus clear the way for financial donations. At Bishnu Charan's insistent effort, Sheth Yugal Kishor Birla and quite a few other wealthy sheths came together at the Birla Bhavan, wanting to see Swamiji demonstrate this extraordinary and inhuman ability. Bishnu Charan and Swamiji came to the event at the appointed time. But nothing was heard about it afterwards. Later, Bishnu Charan disappointedly said in a quiet tone of voice, "Mejda [Yoganandaji] ruined everything. He wasn't able to stop his heart from beating." However, nothing about this was ever brought out. During this time, the writer went one day to see Guru Maharaj in Serampore. Although that particular event was never mentioned anywhere, it was known that Bishtu-da [Bishnu Charan] had organized events for Swamiji in many places, particularly in wealthy Marwari circles. After listening to everything, Gurudev remained quiet for a while and then commented, "He (Yoganandaji) has a disease—where a ghoul comes and sits on his back. First there was Basu-ghoul, and now Bishtu [Bishnu]-ghoul is sitting on his back." Hearing this statement, the writer was completely dumfounded—speechless.

[*Translator's note: "Sheth"—a type of title for a North Indian merchant.]

At one point during this time, Swamiji went to visit Gorakhpur to meet with old relatives and friends. One day, caught up in enacting a childhood memory, he bit into a sugar-cane and accidentally cracked a tooth from the lower mandible. Everyone became flustered by this and Swamiji was eventually taken to the finest dentist in the city, who pulled the broken tooth out and replaced it with a gold one. No news was sent to Calcutta about this. After Swamiji returned to Calcutta, the gold tooth caught the writer's eye, and when he asked about it, Swamiji put his right index finger on his lips and said, "No negative talk!"* Later, he described the above-mentioned event in detail. Then he fell into a pensive mood and said, "God told me, 'Just like this, one day I'll snatch your life from you.'" As Swamiji was saying this he clenched his fist and created an intense expression on his face, and showed how his life was going to be snatched away. Who could have known at that time that he would make his journey into death almost exactly as he said! That account will come later.

[*Translator's note: The quoted statement is in English in the original.]

After Swamiji returned to Calcutta, the writer went with him many times to Serampore to be with Sriguru. There was a time when Swami Satyanandaji and Sailesh-da—Sailesh Mohan—were also with us. One day on the second floor, Sriyukteshvarji was speaking with Yoganandaji; Swami Satyananda was next to him. Standing behind were Sailesh-da and the writer. At one point, Gurudev spoke about the writer, "I love that boy so much. He's a very reasonable* boy." When the writer heard this, there was no end to his joy. He silently said to himself, "Then my outwardly stern Gurudev held a loving place in his heart for this wretched person after all!" Overcome with gratitude for his incredible good fortune, the writer was in ecstasy. And it was this very comment by Sriyukteshvarji that later convinced Yoganandaji to try to get the writer to become a sannyasi and go with him to America. Having received no response whatsoever from the writer, one day Yoganandaji said,

"You don't know what's good for you. Swamiji [Sriyukteshvarji] also feels you're the person." Nevertheless, the writer still remained quiet and was spared from having to state a decision at least for that day. On another day, Ananda-da—Ananda Mohan Lahiri—was with us. It was almost nightfall. Maharaj ji was standing on the upstairs veranda and someone was standing next to him. Ananda-da and the writer were downstairs. Before going upstairs, Yoganandaji went to a drainage spot, a bit apart from the area, and began to urinate into the drainage passage. This caught Gurudev's attention and he cryptically joked, "Yogananda has become a 'paramhansa' [great swan, or great soul]!" After urinating, Yoganandaji saw Ananda-da standing at the front door and quietly said, "Ananda-da! Did you hear? Swamiji [Sriyukteshvarji] called me a 'paramhansa!'" Later, Ananda-da laughed and said to the writer, "You'll see. Yogananda will one day use this title!"

[*Translator's note: The word "reasonable" is in English in the original.]

Sri Sailesh Mohan Majumdar
(Swami Shuddhananda Giriji Maharaj)

Attempt at Uniting Sadhu Sabha and Yogoda Satsanga Society

The days were passing by. Gurudev Sriyukteshvarji began to feel that it was time to take care of the matters which he could not carry out until Yoganandaji returned to India. Gurudev wanted to tie up the issues of the transference of his familial property rights, which included the Karar Ashram in Puri, and the distribution of almost 150,000 rupees worth of liquid finances [savings, or cash]. Once these things were legally settled, he could prepare for his final journey. Among the assets were the beautiful and immense two-storey mansion with surrounding property in Serampore and quite a good amount of abadi [functional]* land in a village in the Hoogly district. The Puri ashram and the previously mentioned finances were already designated for the Sadhu Sabha.** Sriyukteshvarji wished for the Puri ashram to be used for the research and practice of astronomy and astrology, and the finances were to be used to fund that endeavor. He had already begun to set up a kind of observatory on the ashram premises modeled somewhat after the "yantar mantar" types of structures in Jaipur, Delhi and Benares. A nephew of his named Manu lived with Maharaj ji at his Serampore house. This man had no means of income, nor did he do any kind of job. It has been heard that Gurudev wished to leave all of the village land to Manu, and the rest, including Priyadham—his Serampore home, the Puri ashram and the aforementioned savings, to the institution directed by Yoganandaji. Guru and his dear disciple discussed all of this and decided to form a legal deed which would connect all of the organizational branches of India and America under one institution. The responsibility of preparing the paperwork was given to an established attorney by the name of Roy Choudhury from the High Court area. The central organization was to be named "Yogoda Satsanga Society of India and America," with Sriyukteshvar Giri as its founder and Swami Yogananda as its president. On the day the deed was to be witnessed and signed, everyone went to the attorney's office. Guru Maharaj Sriyukteshvarji was driven there by Sananda Lal. Satyanandaji and several others were also present. The agreement stated that Sadhu Sabha and all of the branches of Yogoda Satsanga, including all of the property and funds of both organizations, would be merged as one under a new name. At the time of signing, this came out of Yoganandaji's mouth: "I was really the one who did everything..."—meaning the title of founder, particularly because of America, where the entire institution was founded by him. Sriyukteshvarji Maharaj was shocked; he looked at Yoganandaji's face for a second, took his walking stick and marched out of the attorney's office directly to Sananda Lal's car, and went back. Everyone was absolutely dumbstruck by this sudden and completely unexpected and unimaginable event. Thus Sriyukteshvarji's heart's desire—leaving all that belonged to him to his worthy disciple—was never carried out. Sriyukteshvarji was so wounded by Yoganandaji's behavior at that time that, on that very day, Gurudev gave up all hope of a future for his institution. When the writer met Sananda Lal for the last time in 1978, this event was brought up. Sananda

Lal said at that time, "Swamiji Maharaj [Sriyukteshvarji] was so angry while we were riding in the car that he said, 'That is not self-will; that is unlawful conduct.'"

[*Translator's note: The word "abadi" can mean land ready to be used, farmland, or residential land.]

[**Translator's note: "Sadhu Sabha"—spiritual society founded by Swami Sriyukteshvar Giri.]

Going to the Kumbha Mela

This regrettable state of affairs naturally caused Yoganandaji to become tormented and full of sorrow. However, he himself was responsible for matters turning out this way. No one except those who were present at the attorney's office knew what had happened. Some signs of somberness surely colored his usually cheerful behavior full of life, but those who were not abreast of the things that went on in the private areas of his life could not catch this change in him. Gurudev Swamiji Maharaj had returned to his normal manner of being. There was no indication of there being any difference in the loving behavior he had always demonstrated towards his dear disciple. Yogananda went to see Sriguru several times after the incident mentioned in the previous section; there was no change in the affection and friendliness with which Gurudev had treated Swamiji before. One day, Yoganandaji told Gurudev that he had a great desire to go to the Kumbha Mela [massive gathering of sages] in Prayag, Allahabad. Gurudev sarcastically responded, "What'll you see at the Kumbha Mela? Nothing but hundreds of naga sannyasis [nude sages], ringing their bells while they parade themselves up and down." As Sriguru mentioned the naga sannyasis, he raised his arms and waved his hands, like someone waving from a parade to the crowd. And then Gurudev broke into a huge belly laugh. Yogananda was a bit thrown by Sriyukteshvarji's enactment, but he replied, "But the Kumbha Mela was where you met Babaji Maharaj [Lahiri Mahasaya's immortal Guru]!" Gurudev did not respond further. Perhaps he thought that his parodying act would make Yogananda abandon his ideas about going to that immense conference of religious people. But after returning to Calcutta, Yogananda took some relatives and went to the Kumbha Mela in Allahabad anyway. When word of this got to Sriyukteshvarji, Gurudev could not even believe it at first. With an expression of great disappointment and sadness, he asked the news bearer, "What did you say? Yogananda left?" Sriguru fell into a state of resignation after hearing the news. During the morning, he had come to know that his days in this world were coming to an end, although he did not outwardly tell anyone. All of his efforts to complete things and all of his seeming anxiety about matters at hand were connected to his being aware of this fact. Now, his duties for this part of his journey were finished; it was time for the Return. Without telling anyone, he began to prepare for his final journey. Previously, every year at this particular time, Guru Maharaj used to leave Serampore and hold gatherings at different village centers of Yogoda Satsanga in Midnapore [Medinipur]. He met with disciples there, initiated new aspirants into the path of Kriya Yoga and then went for the annual festival held at the Puri ashram at that time of year. Usually, the date of this celebration was designated to be immediately after the Holi festival [festival attributed to Krishna, where people color each other with vermillion], and those attending were invited to come to the Puri ashram with the remnants of Holi still on them. But this year, Gurudev asked everyone by letter to gather at the Puri ashram before Holi. Before leaving Serampore, he met with those who were closest to him in that town. Near his house was the home of a distinguished brahmin barrister. Sriyukteshvarji was close to most everyone in that family. The present guardian of that house is now quite advanced in years. He remembers Sriyukteshvarji very well. In 1975, he told the writer, "That year [1936], Swamiji Maharaj came to our house and asked us to call my mother-in-law. When mother came out on the second floor veranda and looked at him, covering her head with part of her sari [sign of showing respect], Swamiji Maharaj said to her, 'Bouthan [respected sister], I'm going! All is well, no?' Everyone thought that he was leaving for the Puri ashram for the annual festival, like the years before. But we all realized that seeing people in this way before he left was something different." The old disciples of the different Midnapore branch-centers have said, "We'd never seen Gurudev this solemn. It felt like he had come to see all of his children for one last time." Guru Maharaj arrived at the Puri ashram quite a few days before the Holi festival.

Meanwhile, Swami Yogananda, with several of his relatives and friends, had made his way to the Kumbha Mela—the oldest, most prominent and largest gathering of saints and sages in India. Swamiji collected many anecdotes for his future autobiography here, but the singular thing for which he longed so deeply and intensely—the darshan [holy sighting] of Babaji Maharaj—was not fulfilled. From the lecture that Yoganandaji gave in front of hundreds of people on January 1, 1937, it was learned that Paramhansa Keshabananda indicated to him that if he went to Badrinarayan, there was a possibility of having darshan of Babaji Maharaj. Swamiji returned to Calcutta from the Kumbha Mela visit about one or two days before Holi. Upon returning, he came to know that Gurudev was in Puri and had asked him to go there. But brothers, sisters, relatives and close friends did not want to let him go when, after so many years, they again had a chance to celebrate the joyous festival of Holi with him. And Yoganandaji also could not deny them.

Gurudev's Final Journey

During the day of the Holi festival, everyone was caught up in joyful celebration, coloring each other with vermillion and water-paint; the day was filled with fun and laughter. In the evening, a telegram arrived from Puri, saying that Gurudev was extremely ill and that there was very little chance of his remaining alive. Yoganandaji immediately prepared to go to Puri. Apparently Gurudev had himself written, by his own hand, on the telegram form, "Never so sick before."* It was too late to catch a train for Puri that day; so it was decided that the Puri Express would be taken the very next morning. However, the train was fully booked and no reservations could be made for traveling to Puri on that day. Thus it was on the third day that Swamiji took Richard Wright and Sudhirda—Sudhir Roy—and made for Puri on the Puri Express. But because of this lengthy delay, Yoganandaji was not able to see Sriyukteshvarji alive. When he arrived at the Puri ashram, he saw the elder and close disciples of the past sitting around Sriyukteshvarji's mortal frame and waiting anxiously for Yoganandaji to arrive. All of the elders were there: Roy Bahadur Atul Roy Choudhury, Amulya Santra and Amulya Das and others from Kidderpore, as well as the elder disciples from the various village centers in Midnapore, and more. Everyone was present during Gurudev's last moments except the one who was his representative to the world. Yoganandaji performed the last rites, and, as realized beings are traditionally put under the earth or entombed, and not cremated, Gurudev's body was buried on the premises of the Puri ashram. Guru Maharaj left for his Great Journey on March 9, 1936. Under Yoganandaji's direction, a bhandara celebration [honorary celebration] for this occasion was held, attended by innumerable disciples and devotees from many different places. Yoganandaji initiated Sudhir-da into the path of sannyas, giving him the name of "Swami Sevananda Giri," and turned over the management of the Puri ashram to him.

[*Translator's note: The quoted statement is in English in the original.]

The unfortunate result of the previous effort to unite Sadhu Sabha and Yogoda Satsanga Society made it necessary to re-establish Sadhu Sabha. Swami Yogananda was the deputy-president of Sadhu Sabha; after

Gurudev Sriyukteshvarji's departure, the full responsibility of that sabha [congregation] fell on Swamiji's shoulders. He re-established Sadhu Sabha with himself as president, Swami Satyananda as deputy-president and the late Prabhas Chandra Ghosh as director, and set the association on a new course. Because the order now had a new president, it became necessary to make a legal adjustment regarding the ownership of its assets—such as the Puri ashram and the money designated for the Sadhu Sabha. The Serampore home and the Puri ashram were inherited family-properties. Because Sriyukteshvarji did not have a living offspring, difficulties arose in making decisions about those properties, as those houses and the previously mentioned functional land in a village in the Hoogly District were not left to anyone in a written will. The houses—where for almost half-a-century Sriyukteshvarji initiated aspirants into Kriya Yoga, taught the very essence of spiritual wisdom in many other ways, and kept the places ever-open as second homes for hundreds and thousands of disciples and devotees—were of deep emotional value to his followers for their spiritual atmosphere and memories attached to them. It was because he had foreseen all of these issues that Sriyukteshvarji wanted to merge and re-establish both institutions [Sadhu Sabha and Yogoda Satsanga], legally registered, under one new name. Yoganandaji must now have been regretting his past indiscretion. Swami Satyananda became the acting president of Sadhu Sabha after Yoganandaji went back to America because the signature of an officer of an organization was not legally recognized in India if that officer was residing in, and a citizen of, another country.

Swamiji's Last Chapters in India

The ever-cheerful Yoganandaji's vivaciousness seemed to subside a bit after Gurudev's passing. After having come back to India for Sriguru and having been in his physical presence once again, he had not been able to carry out three of Maharaj ji's last wishes, whatever the reasons may be. Gurudev's wishes were: first—uniting Sadhu Sabha and Yogoda Satsanga as a newly registered institution under a new name, and thereby turning over all of his work legally into the hands of his deserving disciple; second—wanting his dear disciple to stay with him during his last days on Earth instead of going to the Kumbha Mela (perhaps there were some instructions and wisdom that Gurudev wanted to pass on); and third—for guru and beloved disciple to see each other one last time before the end.

Yogananda's pain was only natural and expected, although he did not show any outward signs of it other than being much more introverted than usual. The vision that he had had of working with Bishnu Charan gradually faded and eventually disappeared. The only remnant of that idea was the selection of a master of physical culture from Bishnu Charan's center, Sri Krishna Kali Bandopadhyay—an enterprising man of high character as well as an expert teacher of all sorts of athletic arts, whom Yoganandaji appointed as the director of physical education at the Ranchi center. With the number of days remaining for his stay in India gradually diminishing, Swamiji began to focus on completing whatever organizational work related to India could be finished while he was still in his home country. Swami Satyanandaji remained as the head of the Ranchi ashram. Yoganandaji set up a new board of directors for the Yogoda Satsanga Society of India with himself as president, Prabhas Chandra as deputy-president, Satyanandaji as director of operations, along with Ananda Mohan Lahiri, Prakash Chandra Das and others filling the remaining positions of the board. The very same Tulsi Narayan and Prakash Chandra that Swamiji had, until now, kept apart from any organizational involvement with Yogoda Satsanga, were now recruited to work for the society and that distanced relationship was gone, at least visibly. On other hand, there were no appointees from those members of the graduated students' committee and the Calcutta center who in the past had actually carried the flag of Yogoda Satsanga through all sorts of difficulties, and these aforementioned appointments naturally took all of those previous supporters by surprise. However, Swamiji did have a special place in his heart for this center [Calcutta center and associated students' committee residential quarters]. Because this branch was connected with the residential quarters of the graduated students' committee, he thought of this center as a main base, and he highly approved the course of work that went on at the place. It is possible that he felt a need to make this residence and center a single permanent establishment. His first inclination was, if he had the right, to make one of his father's two houses, or at least part of one of the houses, the permanent place for Yogoda Satsanga in Calcutta. And he stated this wish to his father as well. But because of vehement protests by his younger brothers Sananda Lal and Bishnu Charan, the aged father Bhagabati Charan could not comply. Quite expectedly, this conflict between Swamiji and his two brothers caused a rift between the older one and the younger two for a time. Richard Wright was an observer and witnessed these exchanges, about which he spoke to the writer, and at which time he also expressed his great pain at seeing Bhagabati Charan's condition in the middle of this predicament. At that time, Swamiji did not have much cash available to him. The Ranchi ashram had been purchased with a lump sum, and the cost of staying and traveling in India was incalculable. He did however ask the writer to look for a house that could be immediately bought for a low price. Such a house was looked for and found; the deal was also set; but in the end the seller backed out. Swamiji's heart's desire was to establish a permanent property for the Calcutta Yogoda Satsanga, either in Calcutta proper or on its outskirts, preferably with an expansive garden, and situated somewhat near the banks of the Ganges. The writer and Prakash Chandra found several mansion-properties on the northern edges of the city, but no deal could be finalized. Finally Swamiji left the clever Prakash Chandra with the responsibility of finding the proper place in the future, according to Yoganandaji's specifications. But there was another imperative task that Prakash Chandra was given: making probate arrangements for Yoganandaji to legally become the owner of Sriyukteshvarji's physical, financial and intellectual properties which were previously under the name of Sadhu Sabha, and putting "Priyadham" [Sriyukteshvarji's home] in Serampore under the ownership of Yogoda Satsanga, either the entire premises or at least the surrounding property. Swamiji assigned Prakash Chandra these responsibilities because Prakash Chandra was an expert at handling these court matters, as well as being a man who was very seasoned in materially oriented affairs.

Yogananda had one particular desire—to initiate at least three of the graduated students of the Ranchi Vidyalaya into the path of sannyas according to scriptural injunctions. These three were: Sudhir-da (Sudhir Roy), Panchkori-da (Panchkori De) and the writer. He initiated Sudhir-da into sannyas immediately after Gurudev's departure, giving him the new name of Swami Sevananda Giri. After much coaxing by Swamiji, Panchkori-da agreed to take the name of Brahmachari Shantananda, and the writer somehow got himself to be spared from any of this. So it can be said that fifty percent of Yoganandaji's wish was fulfilled, although a few years later Shantananda went back to using his family name. The responsibility of using the new methods of disseminating Yogoda teachings and initiations from Ranchi—printing and publishing reading material titled "Precepta Lessons" and other such work—was given to Shantananda. Yoganandaji said that he had found this way of teaching to be very successful in America. By this method, aspirants are reached in distant places and taught spiritual practices and, at the same time, the ashram benefits financially. However, it has been seen that the deep attainment one gains after one hears about Kriya Yoga directly from a master and then experiences the teachings first-hand in a private initiation from his/her guru is extremely difficult to realize by this process where a group of people read about the teachings in circulars and letters and then receive initiation en masse; it is also very difficult to teach a spiritual science as substantial as Kriya Yoga by this method. The writer has seen proof of this fact innumerable times. In any case, Swamiji was the first to use this method to spread the teachings of Kriya Yoga. He had said that his American students and disciples of Kriya Yoga numbered more than 150,000 in 1935.

Encounters with Sages

Among the things Yoganandaji needed to accomplish while in India, one of the most significant was gathering information about the miraculous lives of sages and saints. It was known at this time that he had decided to write a book about this subject after he returned to America. Whenever any word would come to him about any extraordinary man or woman of spirituality, he would immediately go and see that person. The writer was with him some of these times. Swamiji particularly wanted to find out more about Babaji Maharaj [Lahiri Mahasaya's immortal Guru]. He had gone as far as the Kumbha Mela to find that great being, only to be unsuccessful and disappointed. One morning, Swamiji took the writer with him to the house of Dr. Mukherjee, a renowned physician of that time in Calcutta, to meet with Sri Bhupendra Nath Sanyal, one of the eminent disciples of Yogiraj Shyama Charan Lahiri. Acharya Sanyal had not himself seen Babaji Maharaj, but he said that he had heard that Babaji Maharaj and the Lord Lahiri Mahasaya looked very similar, only that Babaji Maharaj looked a bit young. Yoganandaji restated this conversation about Babaji Maharaj in his New Year's Day talk in America on January 1, 1937. Nowhere did Swamiji ever say that he saw Babaji Maharaj with his own eyes. Another time, Swamiji learned from the late Sucharu Bhaduri—nephew of Dhirananda—that there was a sage from Chandan Nagar who supposedly knew a great many things about Lahiri Mahasaya's miraculous powers, and through Sucharu-da an appointment was set up to meet this sage inside a glass shop at China Bazar in Calcutta. The time of the appointment was 3 p.m. On the specified day, Richard Wright drove Swamiji, Sucharu-da and the writer to that shop in China Bazar, and an audience was had with that sage inside that store. Tall, impressively built, with a prominent nose and long hair tied in braids, somewhat fair and dressed in the ochre robe of sannyasis [ascetic monks]—the man looked quite like the sages of yore. Wright had remained outside. Swamiji began the conversation in a cordial and gracious manner. When he asked the man whether he knew about the miraculous powers of Lahiri Mahasaya, the man said, "I'm so consumed by my own miracles, when would I have time to know about someone else's?" This answer sounded very "out of tune" to the writer's ears. After some more exchanges, the sadhu [sage] pointed to his foot, saying, "You see—there is no big toe there. I had to sacrifice that to save the life of a devotee who was dying from the poison of snakebite." And we saw that the sadhu's big toe was missing from his left foot. Somewhere during this conversation, the subject of the great saint Bholananda Giri Maharaj came up; he had passed away one or two years before. The sadhu said, "His dead body was lying on a street in Calcutta!" After hearing this, the writer could no longer keep quiet and spoke out, "Really? He passed away in Hardwar! Why would his body be on a street in Calcutta?" Annoyed, the sadhu maharaj said brusquely, "Do you know how many Bholanandas there are? Do you keep informed about all of them?" By that time the writer had surmised the substantiality of this "sage." After this meeting was over, the writer asked Swamiji in the car, "Swamiji! How did you feel about this fellow? I certainly thought he was a 'number one' fraud." Perhaps remembering his initial respectful approach to the man, Swamiji replied, "Look. Whenever I meet with people, I do so completely openheartedly. If they want, it's possible that in the beginning they can cheat or fool me. But when they get caught, they get caught with their hands and legs bound!" Almost a decade later, when the writer was carrying on his life as a worker in the world and living in Chandan Nagar, he found out some interesting things about this particular sadhu. His name does not come to mind. His only son was named Saagasakta Bhanti Thakur. The sadhu had a large house for a temple which contained a shrine. His many disciples—men and women, mostly from villages outside Chandan Nagar, came to see him during festivals and such, when they filled both the temple premises and the sadhu's financial coffer. However, the sadhu had a terrible reputation in the neighborhood. The young people especially despised him. One of them was the young man who was the landlord of the rented house in which the writer lived at the time. When this young man heard the story of the sadhu's big toe from the writer, he could not stop laughing. He said that during one of the "rath" festivals [festival with a parade of chariots], some of the youths of the neighborhood ran a chariot's wheel over the sadhu's foot. The sadhu had to go to the hospital and have his big toe amputated.

At that time, Swamiji also was in the presence of with two women sages in Calcutta, both called by the respectful title of "Ma" [mother]. One was "Bimala-Ma," the wife of the sage Gyan Bhai. They lived in the Ramakrishna monastery of Annada Thakur in Eriyadaha, by the Kali Temple in Dakshineshwar. There was a school in the monastery for celibate women. When Swamiji went to the monastery to visit Bimala-Ma, his welcoming became somewhat of a spiritual gathering [satsang]. Devotional songs and chants were being sung. Bimala-Ma was seated in "virasana" [a yogic seated posture] next to Gyan Bhai. As the rhythm changed in the music, her thighs began to quake and suddenly, she stood up in a mythical religious pose, standing on one leg, with her eyes absolutely transfixed. Gyan Bhai quickly got up and grabbed with both hands so that she would not fall. Her entire body was as stiff as wood; no joint could be bent with any effort. Gyan Bhai carefully laid her down on a carpet right in the meeting room. After quite a while, Bimala-Ma, with a start, began to cry, after which her body became relaxed and normal again. Gyan Bhai said, "Who knows what is happening to Bimala these days. This happens so often now. Sri Sri Thakur had said that every year there will be one new realized being from this monastery!"

The second of these women sages was Sri Sri Anandamoyi Ma. Swamiji came to know about her through Sucharu-da—Sucharu Bhaduri—as well [who had told Swamiji about the sadhu with the missing toe]. Anandamoyi Ma was staying at that time as a guest at a respected and well-to-do family's house on Rasbehari Avenue—known then as Baligunge Avenue—in South Calcutta. Swamiji's car arrived at the house, where about 25-30 devotees had gathered on the sizeable yard outside, and, they, along with members of the household, were standing around Anandamoyi Ma, and chanting "Ma, Ma" with different chant-songs. It goes without saying that the writer was with Yoganandaji. Immediately after Swamiji was seen, Anandamoyi Ma came up to him and said, "Baba! Baba [father]!" and began to express great joy at seeing Yoganandaji. After a short while, Swamiji seated himself on the courtyard itself, and Anandamoyi Ma again spoke out "Baba!" and sat down on Swamiji's lap. After satsang continued for a while, Swamiji left with his companions. Gurudev was still alive when this meeting took place. The second time Swamiji saw Anandamoyi Ma was on the train platform at the station in Serampore. It was about 10 or 11 in the morning. Swamiji was returning to Calcutta after having seen Gurudev. The car was traveling on the road alongside the triangular field next to the station, on the way to G.T. Road. Suddenly, everyone noticed that Anandamoyi Ma was waiting with a few companions on the platform of the station for a train. Procuring some rice flakes mixed with yogurt in a paper container, Swamiji and his assistants quickly parked the car under the platform, ran up the steps and greeted Ma. The conversation with her was again very heartwarming and tender. Swamiji offered her the rice flakes mixed with yogurt. "Baba! Please feed me!" Sri Ma replied. Swamiji said, "Why don't you take it with your own hands? Don't you eat by your own hands?" "You see. Everyone's hands are my hands!" answered Ma. Swamiji fed Ma some of the food and also ate a little himself. It was found out later that Anandamoyi Ma did not eat by her own hands. Swamiji invited her to come to the Ranchi ashram. That invitation was honored some time afterwards. Anandamoyi Ma stayed at the Ranchi ashram, bestowing great joy to all who were there.

In reality, after Gurudev's passing, Yoganandaji became somewhat restless. The desire to go back to dear ones in America also awakened. A time comes to mind when the writer presented a stack of letters to Swamiji and then sat down next to him. The first one he opened was an envelope containing a handwritten missive. The letter was several pages long. After reading it just a bit, Swamiji got up and began to dance, kissing the letter at one spot. He exclaimed, "The fellow must have been an Indian yogi in his past life!" Swamiji allowed the writer to read the part of the letter he was kissing. It was written, "My pen stops…. Everything has become light."* The letter was from Mr. Lynn. It was only natural that the overflowing love and reverence of hundreds and thousands of men and women in America would stir his heart. Athough he had not been able to accomplish all of the things he had planned during his stay in India, the pull for his homeland did not have much gravity any more, now that Gurudev was gone.

[*Translator's note: The quoted statement is in English in the original.]

Journeying Twice to Bombay on the Way to America

It is certain that the pain of not being able to fulfill Gurudev's last wishes gnawed at Yoganandaji from within; this is evidenced by Swamiji's desire that, before he left for America, he would go to each of the village-centers in Midnapore in which Gurudev had left his final footprints. Sriyukteshvarji had visited them all before his death. The actual date of the morning does not come to mind, when Swamiji, with companions Richard Wright and Sister Ettie, took a train on the B.N. Railway line and left Calcutta amidst the tears of the throng of devotees and friends who came to say farewell. One of the strongest memories etched in mind is that of Atin Basu, brother-in-law of Yoganandaji's elder-sister Roma Devi, garlanding Yoganandaji with an enormous garland of lotuses—a wreath which hung down to the feet.

The party reached Bombay. Preparatory activities for the journey were being conducted on the ship. Swamiji's heart was heavy-laden. As he was going to sleep at night at his hotel, suddenly, like a dream, he saw Sriyukteshvarji physically appear in his room. Yoganandaji looked at Gurudev's face and said, "Why are you so disappointed?! Are you offended so much?!" Swamiji retold this statement to the writer later; Nani Bhaya* (Nalini Mohan) was present at the time, along with one or two others; one cannot now recall exactly who they were. After this vision, Swamiji postponed his travel to America for the time being and returned with his assistants to Calcutta. It is true however that on New Year's Day—January 1, 1937, during the first public speech after he went back to America, Yoganandaji described the above-mentioned event as the resurrection of Sriyukteshvarji. A professional in the psychological sciences may say that the vision was a reflection of Swamiji's own pained state of mind. After returning to Calcutta, Yoganandaji fully engaged himself with the work of the organization. Finding a permanent place for the Calcutta center and its associated students' residence was of primary importance. But because of circumstantial issues, efforts were not successful. It was also necessary to take care of the legal matters surrounding Sadhu Sabha and Gurudev's physical, financial and intellectual properties. It was at this time that Swamiji spent a great deal of time with Prakash Chandra. Also, Swamiji still had not forgotten his wish to bring the writer into the path of sannyas. In any case, finally in the middle of September 1936, Swamiji again left Calcutta and resumed his journey back to America. This time he took Nani Bhaya and Tinkori Bhaya—Tinkori De, who was a schoolmate of the writer since childhood and at the Ranchi Vidyalaya as well—with him to Bombay on the Bombay Mail [train] from the Howrah train station. After enjoying a few days in Bombay, Swamiji boarded the ship for America and left India for the last time. His stay in India was for almost exactly one year. But it seemed as if he accomplished one eon's worth of work during this short time. Firmly establishing his message on Kriya Yoga, he flooded everyone, like the Ganges, with new hope, new certainty and new life. The unfathomable depth of Swamiji's love for India and his unshakeable reverence for her is expressed in every rhyme and meter of the poem he composed in America called, "My India." Once, Swamiji told the writer, "India's spiritual wisdom should have her on the highest place in the world, but how materially poor Indians are—so imprisoned by poverty! I wonder if I should go around the world, holding out a beggar's satchel for my country?!" What does a sannyasi have other than his beggar's satchel? Apparently, towards the end of his life, Swamiji used to tell his close American disciples, "I will leave this mortal body while singing the praises of India!" And in terms of actual events, his departure played out exactly like this, word for word. But that account will come later.

[*Translator's note: "Bhaya" is a respectful term meaning "brother," used to address friends of the same age.]

One afternoon after Yoganandaji had returned to America, Swami Satyananda—most probably under attorney's advisement—took the writer, Nani Bhaya, Rohini and Bishan Bose—Rohini's friend—with him to "Priyadham," Sriyukteshvarji's ancestral home in Serampore. Gurudev's nephew Mano cordially invited everyone in. Mano lived in an inner section of the house.

Arrangements were made for the party to sleep in the two living rooms. Food was brought in from a restaurant for the evening meal. The room in which Sriyukteshvarji gave Kriya initiation over the years—renovated by Gurudev before his departure—contained an iron safe. In the evening, Satyanandaji took the writer with him into the room, locked the doors, and opened the safe. There was nothing much within the vault, just a small stack of papers bundled together with a small paper wrapper. That bundle was given to the writer and the safe was again locked. The next day, Satyanandaji entrusted the two front rooms of the second floor to Rohini and Bishan, gave them the funds they needed, and returned to Calcutta with the writer. Nani returned one day later. After just a few days, Rohini and Bishan were back in Calcutta with the news that Mano had brought some people from the neighborhood, forced Rohini and Bishan out of the property, locked the doors from the inside of the house and took over the entire premises. Because the status of Gurudev's ancestral property was not yet settled legally, the house that was a pilgrimage place for hundreds of disciples and devotees was pilfered in this way.

One day at midday at the Calcutta center, the writer found himself both astonished and ecstatic at the same time, when he discovered that the aforementioned wrapped bundle contained a letter that Gurudev had written to the Lord Sri Sri Lahiri Mahasaya, as well as a stack of papers containing abbreviated commentary notes on Chapters 10 through 18 of the Srimad Bhagavad Gita, written in Sriyukteshvarji's own handwriting. The Lord Sri Sri Lahiri Mahasaya's protocol was to return the letters back to the original writer with His answer written on the same pages, along with His signature. The Lord's answer in this letter contained a verse from the Atharva Veda on Shambhavi Mudra. The book of spiritual commentary on the Gita that Gurudev had published during the time the Lord was still playing out His human drama was completed up to the ninth chapter. For the last nine chapters, Sriyukteshvarji had written commentary material in the form of short notes, as mentioned above. In the 1940's, when Sevayatan ashram reprinted and republished Gurudev's Gita, due to the insistence of this writer, the final nine chapters were added to this reprinted version, without adding, taking away or editing the text in any way or form.

CHAPTER 6
The Last Act

Offering by American Devotees for Swamiji's Homecoming

Swamiji's innumerable American devotees had secretly prepared a surprise homecoming* gift for him. On the shores of the Pacific Ocean, in the town of Encinitas, an enchantingly beautiful "Swarna Kamala" [golden lotus] temple was built for him, made possible mostly through the financial help of the sage Lynn and the physical coordination directed by the devoted senior disciple and woman-sage Sister Gyan Mata. This "Swarna Kamala" temple received the highest governmental commendation for architecture above all other structures considered for meritorious recognition by the United States Government that year. There were three immense lotuses built on the roof of the temple. And to keep them from being eroded by the elements of the sea air, the lotuses were plated with gold; this prevented damage from natural forces and maintained the brilliance of the petals at all times. The temple was created with such expertise that when Swamiji would get up on the stage in the meeting space of the temple, he would see nothing but vast blue ocean through the massive glass windows surrounding the room. Having received this wonderful temple, Swamiji remarked, "Another dream of mine has now become manifested." The temple was secluded—apart from other properties, and the meditation chamber was especially serene, where Swamiji and Mr. Lynn would remain in spiritual absorption for many hours. Some time later, the mass of rock on which this structure was founded became eroded by the endless thrashing of waves, and the temple eventually collapsed into the sea. A similar edifice was erected in another location relatively nearby.

[*Translator's note: The word "homecoming" is in English in the original.]

Celebration-gathering with American Devotees; Lynn Named Rajarshi Janakananda and Brahmachari Jotin Named Swami Premananda

Swamiji selected the New Year's Day celebration on January 1, 1937 as the time for his first public address after his return to America. Many distinguished disciples were invited to the joyous occasion, and they came from all over the United States. Among the notable Indian devotees were Brahmachari Jotin, Sri Nerode, Sri Narendra Kumar Das and such others. Dr. Lewis from Boston—one of the oldest supporters of Swamiji, Saint Lynn, Sister Gyan Mata, Sister Sraddha, as well as other devotees from the Mount Washington center were among the American disciples attending. It can be said that it was at this occasion that Lynn was recognized as being in the second position in the hierarchy after Swamiji. A short while after this event, Lynn began to reside permanently at the Mount Washington center, and Yoganandaji bestowed upon him the spiritual name of Rajarshi Janakananda, although he never was formally initiated into the path of sannyas. Swamiji often said that his reason for coming to America was fulfilled by Lynn's presence. Close devotees reverentially said that Swamiji and Lynn were two flames from the same spiritual Light. Also at this time, Swamiji initiated Brahmachari Jotin according to scriptural injunctions into the path of sannyas, giving him the name of "Swami Premananda."

If examined, the speech Yoganandaji gave at that reunion celebration reveals much. The first noticeable thing is that up to that point, he had never used the name "Paramhansa Yogananda"; he was always known previously as "Swami Yogananda." It was in his autobiography that he first makes it known that Gurudev Swami Sriyukteshvarji bestowed the title of "paramhansa" on Yoganandaji while he was in India. However, the writer and others who were close to him were not aware of this happening. Swamiji himself had never mentioned this news to anyone. Any sannyasi [renunciate], sadhu [sage] or brahmachari [celibate aspirant] can be given the title of "paramhansa"; this is one of the wonderful aspects of Hindu culture. Swami Satyanandaji had said, "Yogananda was attracted to the 'paramhansa' title since childhood." One humorous incident comes to mind regarding this. Once at dusk, Swamiji was urinating at a drainage spot in the front alley by Gurudev's house in Serampore. Gurudev was standing on the second floor veranda and speaking to someone when he jokingly remarked, "Yogananda has become a 'paramhansa' [great swan]!" Ananda-da [Ananda Mohan Lahiri] and the writer were standing by the front door of the house. They and Swamiji heard Gurudev's ironic joke. Swamiji came to the front door and said, "Ananda-da! Did you hear? Swamiji [Sriyukteshvarji] called me a 'paramhansa' [great soul]!" Ananda-da softly said to the writer, "You'll see! Yogananda will use this title in the future, for certain." It is not possible to understand why Swamiji did not announce at the speech of New Year's Day in 1937 that Gurudev bestowed this title on him, and why he revealed this only in his autobiography later.

The Picture of Babaji Maharaj

Another point of interest in this reunion speech is Swamiji's references to Mahamuni Babaji Maharaj, the Divine Master of Kriya Yoga. It is clear by this lecture that Yoganandaji did not directly see Babaji Maharaj. Later however, his organization went on propagating a drawing of Babaji Maharaj saying that this is how Swamiji had seen him. This contradiction is astounding and deluding. In truth, there is no similarity with this picture and the description of Babaji Maharaj given by Yoganandaji's Gurudev Sriyukteshvarji, nor is there any similarity in the picture with the descriptions of the Divine Master given by Sri Sri Shyama Charan Lahiri's other senior disciples of old. In 1978, the writer asked Sananda Lal about this matter. He said that his "Mejda" [middle elder brother]—meaning Swamiji—saw Babaji Maharaj at their house on Garpar Road, and that that image of the Divine Master was drawn according to Swamiji's instructions by Sananda Lal. The description of Babaji Maharaj that the writer wrote in his book on Kriya Yoga in English was ascertained from conversations with Sriyukteshvarji, and Sananda Lal concurred that he had also heard Sriyukteshvarji give the same description of Babaji Maharaj [as the writer had heard in his conversations with Sriyukteshvarji]. The March 1937 issue of "Inner Culture," the primary journal of Yogoda Satsanga, contained an article by Swamiji regarding Babaji Maharaj. It seems appropriate to bring it out here, and is presented below:

[Translator's note: The excerpt below, from the March 1937 issue of Inner Culture, is written in English in the original, with a Bengali translation following it. We have only presented the original English verbatim, and not done a "re-translation" of the Bengali translation for obvious reasons.]

Lahiri Mahasaya's Guru

> The great Babaji was the Guru-preceptor of Lahiri Mahasaya. Very little is known about Babaji's life. We hear that he is several hundred years old,

and looks exactly like Lahiri Mahasaya, only much younger in appearance. We are told that once Babaji wanted to give up his body. One of his advanced disciples objected. Babaji reasoned, "What is the difference if I keep a dream body or not? I am alive evermore with or without a body." Then the great disciple of Babaji asked, "Honored Guru-preceptor, if it is the same with you to keep your body or dissolve it in the cosmic stream, why not keep it just for a change?" Babaji answered that he would do so, and vanished. This is why it is said he is never going to give up his physical body.

Swami Keshabananda of Brindaban, disciple of Lahiri Mahasaya, speaks of meeting Babaji in Badri Narayan Himalayas, India. Swami Keshabananda hinted a message from Babaji to me when I visited Keshabanandaji's hermitage in Brindaban, India. Swami Keshabananda especially urged, "Yogananda, sometime you must see Badri Narayan Himalayas, for there I met Babaji."

[Inner Culture—March 1937]

The above article written by Swamiji in his institution's primary journal and his speech on the 1ˢᵗ of January 1937 shows that at least up until that time he had not seen Babaji Maharaj directly. Swamiji did not again come to India as well, so the issue of going to the Himalayas and Badri Narayan cannot even be brought up. Yoganandaji was a man who lived in the world of imagination and spiritual feelings. He saw some things directly and some things with the eyes of his feelings. Towards the end, he often did not perceive a difference between the two. In any case, in the perspective of a historical biographer, there is no believable evidence that the propagated picture of Babaji Maharaj was drawn from having seen the Divine Master directly.

Brahmachari Premeshwarananda or Swami Vinayananda Giri

The change in the mode and direction of work at the main center in Ranchi necessitated new workers to join the organization. At this time, a young man named Sachin Chakrabarty began working for Yogoda Satsanga. Although he was not highly educated, he had worked in Bharat Sevashram for a while, which gave him some general familiarity with the ways and needs of a spiritually oriented institution. But behind it all, the man's main reason for joining Yogoda Satsanga's workforce was to be a part of an internationally powerful organization, and his primary and ultimate goal was to go to America. When he came into contact with the writer in Calcutta, Sachin Chakrabarty immediately asked about the possibilities of working with the

Ranchi center, as well as bringing up the subject of traveling to America several times.

After joining the Ranchi center, he began to write a steady stream of letters to Yoganandaji, hoping to gain Swamiji's trust. Sachin was being secretly encouraged in this endeavor by Prakash Chandra. Prakash Chandra was in charge of carrying out some important work in India for Yoganandaji, but he had no time or place for the old workers and supporters of the organization— far be it for him to have any respect for them whatsoever. He observed that the veteran workers of Yogoda Satsanga were all students and followers of Swami Satyananda. In order to diminish Swami Satyananda's influence, it was necessary to concoct some unflattering and distorted information about him and the veteran workers, and have this slanderous news reach Yoganandaji. Expert and experienced at worldly affairs and conspiracy, Prakash Chandra easily had Sachin on his side. He told Sachin that in exchange he would try to get him to America via Swamiji. The first evidence that this conspiratorial effort was bearing fruit was seen when Satyanandaji received a letter from Yoganandaji asking him to initiate Sachin into the vows of a brahmachari [celibate aspirant] with the new name of Brahmachari Premeshwarananda. Brahmachari Premeshwarananda did not have to stay long in India after his renunciate initiation. Yoganandaji had him go to America, and initiated him there into the path of sannyas [full renunciation], giving him the name of Swami Vinayananda. However, Swami Vinayananda [Sachin Chakrabarty] was not able to stay in America for long.

Swami Yogananda's youngest brother Bishnu Charan went with his future son-in-law Buddha Bose to Swamiji's ashram in America. Within only a few days, Bishnu Charan saw many incidents of unbecoming and suspicious behavior by Vinayananda and made Yoganandaji aware of these, after which Yoganandaji's perception of Vinayananda completely changed. Vinayananda then became a problem for Yoganandaji. The open-hearted and love-filled Yoganandaji did not have an easy time when he had to make harsh and stern decisions against someone. At the same time, he also could not take the chance of a troublesome Vinayananda causing problems for him in America. In the end, Vinayananda was sent back to India with the title of "president" for the Yogoda Satsanga in India. This way, the American part of the organization was free of any more complications from this situation. However, this arrangement certainly caused noticeable discontent to rise in the Indian part of the organization, which eventually resulted in the formal resignation of several distinguished members of the workforce of Yogoda Satsanga in India.

No further efforts were made to take any more brahmachari workers to America from India. Other than a few Indians in the United States, the many American men and women who became part of the workforce of Swamiji's Yogoda Satsanga—who demonstrated great reverence for the practice of Kriya Yoga and devotion towards Swamiji—greatly aided the work of propagating the message. Quite a few men and women among these have taken it upon themselves [separated from Yogoda Satsanga] to spread Paramhansa Yogananda's yogic teachings and yogic message in different citites, guided by their own spiritual realizations.

Publishing His Autobiography

Within a few years after his return to America, Yogananda published his world-renowned book, "Autobiography of a Yogi." It has already been mentioned that he was gathering information on the wondrous and miraculous lives of yogis and realized beings of India while he was in his homeland; he wanted to bring out these accounts to the masses. This extensive work, written in his naturally fluent and moving English, immediately stirred an awakening world-wide. Within a short time, this book was being published in 56 languages. However, translations in Bengali and other Indian languages came much later.

Filled with stories of the miraculous, this book is actually a reflection of Swamiji's own miraculous state of being—his own divine and miraculous life. Although, when examined with an investigative eye, many of the accounts could have been caused by ordinary means, nevertheless, in Swamiji's perception, all happened supernaturally. To the observers around the world of extra-rational and extra-sensory phenomena, this unparalleled book became known as the authoritative work to have such events on record.

Resolute Faith in Kriya Yoga

It was stated at the very beginning of this life-portrait that the heart-oriented way of being was Swami Yogananda's primary trait. No where else in this world could this quality have found such fertile ground for expression than the naturally open atmosphere of America. For this reason, the men and women of America very easily took Yogananda in as one of their own. If anyone would come into contact with him just once, that person would, for the rest of his life, hold Yogananda in the highest place of reverence. Many of the old devotees left in Yoganandaji's absence, but in the end, he was held as a king in their hearts, and this continues to be so. His magnanimous, free-flowing love and joyous spiritual radiance was completely integrated—a perfect match—with the ways of American life. In his book "Hinduism Invades America," Professor Wendell Thomas of the University of Illinois speaks highly of Yogananda spreading his message in America using such a novel and appealing approach. The professor said, "Yogananda completely dove into the American way of life!"* However, he also did not let his commentary go without some words of caution, saying, "Whether the message changes to something else in the end remains to be known."** But there is a great deal of evidence that shows that the essential message did not change. Behind every effort by Yogananda was the root purpose of attracting men and women to Kriya Yoga, no matter what the means. If people were captivated by feats of ordinary mental power—no harm in that; let it be so. Or there could be other ways by which people could be drawn. Swamiji's reverence for Kriya Yoga was profound and deep. While in India, he once told the author, "If Kriya can enter in, in any way whatsoever, then it's all over!" Swamiji felt and said that the Comforter,*** Whom Lord Jesus Christ said would come after him, is the path of Kriya Yoga—the "messenger of Peace." The discontent expressed at times by some older Kriyavans in India at Yogananda's "lightweight" ways of spreading Kriya Yoga comes from fearing a degeneration and disappearance of Kriya Yoga's original methods.

[* and **Translator's note: These quoted statements from Wendell Thomas' book are in Bengali in the original manuscript. What is presented here is a translation of the Bengali and not the original English from the book.]

[***Translator's note: The word "Comforter" is in English in the original manuscript.]

The author came to know about an interesting incident regarding this. Yogananda had met a man by the name of Shelly Trimmer. Shelly was an adept practitioner of mysticism. His knowledge of the mystical arts covered practices from Israel, Egypt—many parts of the world, and the practice of mysticism was his profession in a way. When they met, Swamiji said, "You know mysticism. Teach me mysticism and I will teach you Kriya!" Although Shelly was very spiritual, he was not someone who blindly believed in anything. But he was quite taken by Swamiji's warm and inviting behavior. At Swamiji's request, one day Shelly gave him a demonstration of mystical prowess. In due time, he received Kriya Yoga initiation and began to reside at the Mount Washington center. Yoganandaji had wished that he would remain unmarried and stay in the ashram forever, but this was not a satisfactory proposition for Shelly. He left the ashram some time later. He married and is carrying on his life independent of the organization. To this day, he expresses deep reverence and devotion towards Swami Yogananda; to this day, he practices Kriya Yoga as he learned it from Swamiji directly. The genuine and boundless love from Swamiji's heart strongly resonated with the American people; on top of that was the example of his extraordinarily divine life.

In the 1940's, Swamiji once had Prabhas-da—Prabhas Chandra Ghosh, copresident of Yogoda Satsanga Society in India—and Prakash Chandra go to America. When Prabhas-da returned, he told the writer, "You cannot know how deeply the Americans love and respect Swamiji unless you see it with your own eyes. His presence to them is like that of a king. They love, respect and care about him like a god. You cannot even imagine it!" If the essential inner magnetism within him was not as profound and as sweet as it was, this kind of caring and adoration would truly be unimaginable. As much as Yoganandaji did not have organizational expertise, his personality and heart-attracting power held his innumerable spiritually-oriented devotees in loving embrace. Those who were always close to him could also fulfill their own personal and particular wants because of Swamiji's naturally trusting and affectionate nature; this is not at all difficult to surmise. Those who wrote sweetly worded letters, appealing to his open nature, and expressed what they wanted were able to get things done according to what they each desired for themselves. The end result of this was that in both America and India many devotees and followers moved away from having any connection with the organization, although their love for Swamiji remained ever intact. Towards the end of the 1940's, Swami Yogananda paid less and less attention to the work of the ashram and the organization; he remained much of the time in seclusion, absorbed in sadhana [spiritual practice or meditation]. Janakananda kept himself immersed in sadhana as well. Yoganandaji had also prepared a legal will, to go into effect after his passing, turning over the leadership of the organization to Janakananda.

A solitary and secret cottage was set up where Swamiji sat in meditative rapture for much of the last part of his life. Only one or two of those he trusted the very most knew of the whereabouts of this place. Often, when he would return from the cottage, he would be in a highly-intoxicated state of spiritual bliss and not fully in touch with the world. An American sannyasi disciple of his named Swami Kriyananda Giri had once said, "One day, Swamiji [Yoganandaji] was returning from the cottage, but he could not walk on his own from the intoxication. We had to hold him up as we walked." Swami Kriyananda was carefully holding him and helping him walk. Yoganandaji was saying, "Where am I? I am animating so many bodies! Where am I going?" This happened regularly during his last days. The secret cottage's code name was "29th Palm." Only those who were the closest to him knew. It has been heard that the place was situated somewhere by the edge of a desert area.

In 1951, Swamiji's friend and devout disciple of many years, Sister Gyan Mata—who was senior most in age among the residents of the ashram—left her body. For twenty-six years, since 1925, she was the life-current of the ashram. After her departure Swamiji had said, "Gyan Mata is gone. I also won't be here much longer." During these days he often let those who had been close to him throughout the years know that he would not stay in his body for too many more days. He also would say that after he left, Janakananda would not remain in his body for very long either. Among the thousands of American followers and devotees, particularly three—Dr. Lewis from Boston, Sister Gyan Mata and Rajarshi Janakananda—shined brilliantly as Swamiji's spiritual legacy, having attained high levels of spiritual realization through their reverent and devout discipline. Dr. Lewis had come into Swamiji's life almost immediately after Swamiji arrived in America, and although he was not an ashram resident, he always stood by Swamiji, inconspicuously like a shadow, giving him strength and support at all times. Dr. Lewis also did not take on any matters of significance in his personal and family life without Swamiji's consent.

His Final Journey

1952 was a monumental year. For Yogoda Satsanga, it was a year that brought an era to a close. The newly independent India's first ambassador to America—Binay Ranjan Sen—was planning to visit California with his wife. Many Indians lived in this state, and there was no end to their joy at India finally being a sovereign nation again. These Indians decided that they would put on a gala event to welcome the first ambassador. A welcoming committee was formed and Yoganandaji—being one of the earliest Indian inhabitants of California and one who was revered by everyone—was selected as the head of the committee. Swamiji told some of those who were close to him that this public gathering may be his last. For some time, signs in his manner of talking and behavior hinted that he was perhaps hearing within himself the call to "go back." As he got on the stage at the gathering and was walking towards his seat, Srimati Sen, the wife of the ambassador, came up to Swamiji and touched his feet in pranam [humble salutation]. Friend Nirindra Chandra De (Swami Vidyananda) has rightly written: who could have known that that pranam was the final pranam to this extraordinary being who was a beacon of India's spiritual ideals—a light to the men and women of a newly awakened India?

The final speaker of the occasion was Swami Yogananda. The audience was spellbound by his powerful and soul-stirring words. He constantly pointed out India's pre-eminence in spirituality and her bounty of spiritual treasure, and said that India was the only "land of dreams," the place where he was supremely blessed to have been born, and that if he had to incarnate again, he wished to be born again in that holy country. At the end of the talk, he gave a moving recitation of the poem "My India," which he had composed many years before. Every verse was filled with love and devotion for his country, praising with overflowing reverence the incomparable wellspring of spiritual wealth that is India. After the recitation, the hall exploded with ecstatic applause, and as Swamiji went to take his seat, suddenly, his body collapsed on the stage, touching the seat on the way down. He had been suffering from high blood pressure for some time. The body could not contain the torrential flow of feelings any more. Swamiji expired his last breath in that very place. This unbelievable scene at the gathering was like lightning striking with no clouds in sight. But there was no more that could be done. The child of the Eternal had rejoined the current of the Eternal. The premonition that Swamiji had had during the incident of the sugar-cane and the broken tooth seemed to now have manifested. It seemed that the Lord of All had snatched away his life exactly like that.

His Dead Body Remains without Decay for Many Days

Even after his departure, Swamiji's dead body remained without decaying for twenty-one long days. The district in which he was buried had no record of any other such happening in the one hundred years of records kept for burials. No one knows whether any such account can ever be found even in the history of the world. In 1957, when the author asked Sister Daya about this matter, she said, "It was as if Swamiji was simply lying in a deep sleep, just like he used to lie down to sleep when he was alive. There was no sign of any kind of decay in any part of the body. On the twenty-first day, a white spot was seen on the tip of the nose—the first sign of flesh beginning to decompose. Then we buried his body without any further delay."

CHAPTER 7
Epilogue

Yogiraj Sri Sri Lahiri Mahasaya
Guru of Swami Sriyukteshvar

From 1920 to 1952 Yogananda's life-drama played out mostly in America. If these thirty-two long years are divided in two segments, it is seen that the first part—from 1920 to about the middle of 1936—was filled with the many different facets of propagation, hard work and incessant effort to spread the message, and the second segment—from 1937 to 1952—was in a way spent in preparation for his Final Exit. His entire life was directed by an unseen Power and led by an unseen Hand. If one deeply examines Yogananda's life from his birth to his last breath, one cannot at all escape concluding that he was simply an instrument operated by this unseen Hand—a willing, enthusiastic and dedicated* instrument.

[*Translator's note: The word "dedicated" is in English in the original.]

After Swami Yogananda's departure, according to his will, Rajarshi Jana-kananda became the head of all of Yogoda Satsanga—America, India and all of the branches in the world. Upon assuming his post, Janakananda announced in the first meeting led by him that the only one the congregation would ever recognize as guru would be Paramhansa Yogananda. Neither Janakananda nor anyone following him would ever be guru. Janakananda's devotion towards his guru was incomparable. Ever connected in spirit with his master, his every step was directed by Sriguru. Recently, the writer heard from an American devotee about a wondrous experience that an American disciple of Yoganandaji had had with Janakananda. From the time he was a young boy, this disciple used to go to see Yoganandaji. And whenever he would get ready to leave, Yoganandaji would place some small change in the boy's hand and say, "Buy some chocolate and enjoy it!" Whenever the boy would come, Yoganandaji would give him some small money in this way before he left. After Swamiji's passing, this disciple, now a man, had gone to the ashram and met with Janakananda, and as he was about to leave, Janakananda stopped and closed his eyes for a few moments and then said, "Wait! Guruji just told me to give you a little money." Saying this, Jana-kananda pulled out a small amount of money from his pocket and placed it in this disciple's hand—just like Swamiji used to do when this man was a young boy!*

[*Translator's note: This account of the "chocolate money" was written by Sri Sailendra Bejoy Dasgupta in 1983.]

Just as Swamiji had predicted, Janakananda did not remain in the mortal world much longer. After Janakananda's departure, again as Swamiji's will had provided, Sister Daya became the head of the Yogoda Satsanga of both India and America [the entire organization]. Under her leadership, Yogoda Satsanga gradually went through many changes. Many of the men and women who were older disciples of the order either removed themselves from the central organization or were forced out—not only in America but in India as well. Swami Premananda went his own way; his organization adopted a somewhat different name from the original organization. Swami Kriyananda Giri, who was once the assistant director of Yogoda Satsanga, also left. Others who left were Roy Eugene Davis, Sri Nerode, Shelly Trimmer, older men and women who were respected initiators, and many more. Swami Vinayananda and Swami Atmananda were relieved of their posts with Yogoda Satsanga in India. Although Swami Satyananda did not officially end his association, he went on to live as the head "acharya" [teacher] in Sevayatan, an ashram in Jhargram, Midnapore, founded by some of his followers, as well as a few graduate students from the Ranchi Brahmacharya Vidyalaya, and with the financial patronage of Swami Premananda. All of the people mentioned above became engaged in the spread of Kriya Yoga as they saw fit, according to their personal spiritual understanding.

Currently, Hindu spiritual culture is being spread throughout America in a great number of ways. It cannot be denied that the above-mentioned Kriya Yoga associations fall in that same category of spiritual groups. Even at the time professor Wendell Thomas' book "Hinduism Invades America" was published—in 1930, at least five hundred swamis or spiritual leaders were known to have been engaged in as many different ways of spreading Hindu spirituality there. Since that time, particularly after the independence of India, many more spiritual advocates have joined in the same endeavor in that country. Among them are: Maharishi Mahesh Yogi—teaching transcendental meditation, Srimad Bhaktivedanta Tirthaswami—propagating the word of Sri Krishna Consciousness, Bal-yogi, Bal Bhagavan, Bhagavan Rajneesh and such other well known persons. The West Coast of America, particularly the state of California, is a veritable founding ground for these various types of teachings. Even if Yogoda Satsanga is not the way chosen by every seeker, the name of Paramhansa Yogananda continues to this day to be revered by thousands of American men and women, regardless of organizational affiliation, as befitting that of a saint. Following is some information on those who had learned Kriya Yoga from Yogananda and are carrying on the teachings according to their personal spiritual understanding.

Swami Premananda: It has been previously mentioned that in 1928, the founder of the graduated students' committee of the Ranchi Brahmacharya Vidyalaya, Sri Jotindra Nath Bandopadhyay—first known as Sri Jotin, later as Brahmachari Jotin, and finally as Swami Premananda—was appointed by Yoganandaji as head of the Washington, D.C. branch of Yogoda Satsanga in America. Yoganandaji also assigned Swami Premananda the respected position of International Secretary of Yogoda Satsanga. For such a distinguished disciple to move away from the central organization—or to be forced out—is certainly a regrettable matter. When Sister Daya came to India 1957 as the new leader of the institution, the author went with Nani Bhaya (the late Nalini Mohan Majumdar) to see her at Yogoda Satsanga's villa in Baranagar (part of greater Calcutta). Also present at that meeting were Prabhas-da (Prabhas Chandra Ghosh—the co-director of the Satsanga), and the late Vinay Dube, a young man of impressive stature. When Daya was asked about Premananda's separation from the organization, she said, "One day, a letter addressed to Swamiji (Yoganandaji) came from Washington, D.C. As his personal secretary, I used to open most of his letters and read them first if Swamiji was not present. Because Swamiji was not there that day, I opened the letter and saw that it was written by Swami Premananda. There was an improper statement about Swami Sriyukteshvarji in the letter. As soon as I read that, I became very worried about the kind of effect that comment would have on Swamiji (Yoganandaji), and I closed the letter without going further. I placed it under Swamiji's pillow as was the usual practice. Swamiji arrived, opened the letter and immediately became extremely somber. He asked me, 'Did you read this letter?' With great trepidation, I said, 'Yes. I opened it and read it.' He replied, 'I'm extremely sad that you read this letter!' After remaining quiet for a while, Swamiji said, 'When I am not here, you all should cut off all association with all of these people!' We look upon Sriyukteshvarji, Lahiri Mahasaya and Babaji as God; we worship them and are devoted to them. You can certainly imagine the state of mind this type of offensive statement [in the letter] can cause!" Presently, Swami Premananda is past the age of eighty, and remains established in Washington, D.C., owning the property on which he has a temple, meeting hall and residence. It comes to mind that around 1930-31, he had sent to the Calcutta center a picture of Babaji Maharaj, as perceived in the mind in a spiritually absorbed state, drawn by one of his devotees. Respected by the elite and eminent in the very capital of the United States, Swami Premananda is carrying on the work of spreading Indian spirituality, Kriya Yoga and philosophical knowledge.

Sri Nerode became engaged in Yoganandaji's propagation of Kriya Yoga in the first part of the 1930's. He was one of the distinguished members of Yogoda Satsanga when Swamiji was alive. He is also advanced in age. Currently, he lives near Chicago and gives Kriya Yoga initiation independently. It was in America itself that Sri Nerode met Yoganandaji and came under his influence.*

[*Note: Sri Nerode passed away in year 1983.]

Roy Eugene Davis is one of the most noteworthy of Yoganandaji's disciples. He has no connection with Mount Washington or Yogoda Satsanga. He carries on his work through his foundation in the state of Georgia in America called "Center for Spiritual Awareness." He has a great number of spiritually aspiring followers and devotees in many parts of America and Europe, where there are branches of his institution as well. Well known for his erudite speech and writing, Roy Davis' many books are read in all circles. Paramhansa

Yogananda is the "lord of his heart."* He does not pay much respect towards the work that Yoganandaji's institution carries out at the present time. He has visited India several times—to see Bhagavan Sai Baba.

[*Translator's note: The quoted statement is in the original.]

Swami Kriyananda is an American sannyasi [ordained renunciate] disciple of Yoganandaji. During Yoganandaji's life, he lived at the Mount Washington center, and towards the end of Yoganandaji's life, Kriyananda became one of Yoganandaji's closest associations. He also has many followers in Europe and America. He has written an autobiography as well. Many supernatural experiences related to Yoganandaji are written about in this book. He too has visited India several times, given lectures in certain cities here, and met with Sai Baba as well. Kriyananda has no regard for the present leadership of Yogoda Satsanga, but has immense devotion and reverence for Yoganandaji. His main center is in Nevada City, California.

Goswami Kriyananda is a disciple of a disciple of Swami Yogananda. He too is American. It's possible that his name is self-given. He is a formidable astrologer, by which he makes a good income. He has a center called "Temple of Kriya Yoga," located in Chicago, Illinois. He also gives Kriya Yoga initiation independently.

The "Amrita Foundation" is an institution based in Dallas, Texas. Its representatives have endless respect for Yoganandaji, whereas they have no respect at all for the present leaders of Yogoda Satsanga. It has been mentioned previously that the present heads of Yogoda Satsanga have, on their own, made a great number of changes to Swami Yogananda's original Precepta Lessons, through which Swamiji spread the teachings of Kriya Yoga. The Amrita Foundation claims that they use the original Precepta Lessons for their membership.

An elderly American woman named Yogacharya Aishwarya* lives in the city of Seattle, in the northwestern part of the United States. She was previously engaged in the work of the original Yogoda Satsanga. Currently she gives Kriya teachings on her own in that part of America [northwest].

[*Translator's note: The name is unclear in the Bengali transliteration. Sri Dasguptaji is most likely referring to Yogacharya Mother Hamilton.]

Thus, although Paramhansa Yogananda is greatly revered and honored in America, not all practitioners of the path belong to one organization; on the contrary, the original organization's power and influence have greatly diminished over the years. In India, it is often seen that when a spiritual master passes away, issues arise in the congregation, the result of which is often a splintering of the organization into other independent ones. The same is also seen in America. It is obvious that the reason for such a course of events is because of the lack of an appropriate successor. On top of that, taking advantage of Yogananda's massive popularity through the country, disciples of little stature now present themselves as separate spiritual teachers; this facilitates a way for them to have substantial financial gain as well.

How Kriya is Taught in America

In order to spread Kriya Yoga, Paramhansa Yogananda adopted several variations to the original methods, upon seeing the average Westerner's limitations in physical capacity [for environmental reasons and not innate ones] regarding the carrying out of yogic practices. One indispensable part of yoga sadhana [yogic practice] is "asana" [sitting posture], and in Kriya Yoga, another element is indispensable regarding higher levels of the practice—Khechari Mudra, upon which all of the advanced levels of Kriya are based. In both of these cases, many of the ordinary Westerners are not capable of carrying out these aspects of the practice properly. On the other hand, their sincere desire to know and the fathomless depth of their reverence cannot be questioned. Because of these conflicting factors, Yogananda adopted a few different methods which no doubt produce results; however, it is not possible through these new methods to fully attain that which is spoken of in the scriptures in terms of Kriya Yoga.

In the Patanjal Yoga Sutras, the third limb of "ashtanga" yoga [eight-limbed yoga] is "asana." And "asana" is defined as "a stable and comfortable sitting posture." Since time immemorial, "padmasana" [lotus position] has been the asana instructed for use in the practice of Kriya Yoga.* However, most Americans or Europeans are not able to sit in this posture. For this reason, Yogananda said that sitting on an armless chair, with the legs hanging and the back straight, will also do. Most practicing American Kriyavans [Kriya practitioners] perform Kriya Yoga in this type of sitting position on a chair.

[*Translator's note: A footnote is indicated by the author at this spot. The footnote: "See the author's book on Kriya Yoga."]

The central or fundamental Kriya is the "Hansa" mantra manifesting in the form of pranayam [mystic yogic breathing]. Because of Yoganandaji's method of initiating many people at once, or because of having to learn the teachings from the Precepta Lessons, quite a few misunderstandings can come about. This has been seen in many of the practitioners in both India and America. It is imperative to correct these errors through the direct company of one's guru. Going further, one is only fit to practice the higher Kriyas after one accomplishes Khechari Mudra. This absolutely essential technique is also not very easy to attain. For this reason, Yogananda gave instructions for higher Kriyas even without Khechari. In the perspective of pure Kriya practice, this is not proper; and furthermore, the purpose of practicing higher Kriyas cannot be brought to fruition without Khechari. It seems that because of perceiving this fruitless possibility, "mental kriya" [mental practice] was given the emphasis in the Precepta Lessons. Mental practice is also a practice of scriptural injunction; however, the second, third, fourth and such higher Kriyas cannot ever be varied by methods such as that [mental kriya]. From the second Kriya onward, all of the higher Kriyas must be performed with Khechari Mudra. Without Khechari, neither "Thokar" Kriya nor "Omkar" Kriya can be performed; if anyone says otherwise, then he is not speaking about Kriya Yoga. Mental practices are proper for many other paths. But it is impossible to ever accomplish the distinctive aspects of Kriya Yoga via that method [mental kriya].

In 1930, in his book "Hinduism Invades America," Professor Wendell Thomas had written, "There are five hundred 'swamis' (Hindu spiritualists) living in America, who teach five hundred different spiritual paths."* More than half a century after that statement was published, it is needless to say that this number of spiritual teachers has increased exponentially. Noteworthy among these are Maharishi Mahesh Yogi, Prabhupada Bhaktivedanta Siddhanta, Swami Rama Tirtha, Bal Bhagavan, and finally Bhagavan Rajneesh. All of these teachers teach some sort of mental method of meditation or concentration and such. With the changes taking place in the teaching of Kriya Yoga today—how different Kriya practice remains from these other paths is a matter of concern. The performance of Kriya is one of effort, adherence to accurate discipline, and reverence. Is "Kriya" [work] itself about to disappear, because of the need to find an easier way? Maharishi Mahesh Yogi's "Transcendental Meditation," Prabhupada's "Sri Krishna Consciousness" and other such ways are part of a different kind of spiritual practice. "Yogananda has fully dived into the American way of life. Who knows if the essential message of the teaching itself will change in the end!"** This statement towards the end of the book [Hinduism Invades America] is of course not coming from a respectful heart fearing a turn for the worse; this is a statement of condemnation! That this statement is not appropriate is aptly proved by the incredibly honorific way that the whole of America sees Yoganandaji. Even though his personally founded institution has expanded outwardly, many spiritually thirsty and knowledgeable American men and women of high character are determined to keep Yoganandaji's persona untarnished to this day.

[*Translator's note: The quoted statement is a translation of the Bengali version of the statement from Wendell Thomas' book.]

[**Translator's note: Same as footnote "*" above.]

One undeniable fact is this: By teaching his particular way of Kriya practice and spreading it at a torrential pace throughout and beyond the North American continent, Yoganandaji has completely mixed the methods that are easier for Americans to practice and understand with the original and pure methods and techniques. And the possibility of practicing wrongly or being misdirected has remained. However, it also cannot at all be doubted that Yogananda's three decades of teaching has brought about immense respect and reverence from Americans for the ancient spiritual practices of India. If his personal method of teaching Kriya is to be judged, only two or three disciples or devotees need be pointed out in order to bring the matter to light. Rajarshi Janakananda's spiritual stature has been focused upon earlier. Boston's Dr. Lewis' name has also been mentioned several times, but the level of his spiritual depth can be understood by the account of his final journey. When he gathered that the end was near, Dr. Lewis called all of his family to him, asked them to sit, perform Kriya, and pray. And then he sat on his bed in a yogic posture, withdrew his breath, drew his life force upward and left his body—just the same as an advanced Indian yogi would leave his body at death! Sister Gyan Mata was also an advanced practitioner.

It must be remembered that the script of Yogananda going to America was written by his own guru Swami Sriyukteshvar, following the indications given to Sriyukteshvarji by Mahamuni Babaji Maharaj—the Divine Being of Kriya Yoga. Thus, that Yogananda was animated by a great unseen Power since his childhood is actually not such an astonishing fact. His childhood friend Swami Satyananda used to say that Yogananda was a "Kshanajanma Purush" [person born for the needs of the time]. Every aspect of his life—every situation and every step—bears out this extraordinary fact. It is absolutely certain that, through his presence and propagation, he prepared the ground for a spiritual harvest in America; he openhandedly spread the seeds about as well. Perhaps more care and assistance is necessary now to bring about the intended fruition. There is evidence that this need for help is being felt in America itself. Because of the teachings given out by the Indian or American teachers or gurus in that country today having little resemblance to the methods taught by Yogiraj Shyama Charan Lahiri, it is necessary to have new teachers or gurus. Teachers from within American Kriyavans themselves will rise to fulfill this need; the author believes this to be so, because there is a great lack of teachers or gurus of such a high level in India. As far as one can see, the practice of pure Kriya Yoga has taken root on the spiritual soil of America. It has been found that there are one or two intensely willing, fully dedicated and completely reverential Kriyavans [from America], who have given their entire lives—body, mind and all—to master the practice taught by Yogiraj Lahiri Mahasaya. The blessings of the guru-disciple lineage are certainly showering upon these illuminated beings.

Yogananda did not take birth only for the purpose of intense spiritual absorption. The many supernatural experiences that occurred in his life firmly convinced him that he was a maker of history in his previous incarnations, as well as having been persons of formidable power. He came to know these things in transcendental states. He had said that he was in fact the historical British figure "William the Conqueror." The well-known historical account of William landing on the shores of England and prostrating and kissing the ground—Yoganandaji experienced this within him in a spiritually absorbed state. In 1935, when he and his party were visiting England during the journey back to India, Yoganandaji and Richard Wright were at the palace at Westminster. Yoganandaji said to Wright, "You walk behind me. Immediately after I enter the palace, I will tell you which room is where before we ever get there; you'll see, everything will match up!" Wright said later that Swamiji was right every time about the location of the different rooms. Swamiji himself was there at the telling of this event, and Wright was bearing witness to Swamiji's description of the incident. There was no sense of any kind of "but" in Swamiji's behavior at all! Apparently, in yet another life, he was a vicious and murderous desert marauder. While describing this, Swamiji shivered with horror from time to time, although he maintained a slight smile on the outside. Swami Satyanandaji had said that before Yoganandaji went to America and was living at the Ranchi Brahmacharya Vidyalaya, one night, he screamed out from his room. He said that a cot penetrated through his closed door and a horrific being was seated upon that cot. From that time on, a student would sleep in a separate cot in his room.

Yoganandaji said that if he slept alone, he saw many different beings, and some of the times he woke up in fear.

Engrossed in deep spiritual absorption, Yogananda led an extraordinary life full of contemplative imagination and feeling, and if seen in a certain way, he led a miraculous life. The leadership of people was his prowess, and his faith in the Unseen Power was immense. Even if there were problematic issues in the everyday life of the waking state, besides being one of the great luminary children of Mother India, Swami Yogananda bestowed unending spiritual beneficence to the people of the world as an adept torchbearer of Spiritual Light. Offering, with complete humility, endless reverence, love and prostrations to his memory, I now draw the curtain on this rendition of his life-portrait and my reminiscences of being in his company.

"Dadu"

Acharya Sri Sailendra Bejoy Dasgupta
(1910–1984)

Exalted direct disciple of Swami Sriyukteshvar Giriji Maharaj

Dadu,
We are your children surrendered at your feet. Thank you for guiding us
with your light.
Please accept our quiet offering.

TITLES AVAILABLE FROM YOGA NIKETAN:

The Scriptural Commentaries of Yogiraj Sri Sri Shyama Lahiri Mahasaya:
Volume 1

The Scriptural Commentaries of Yogiraj Sri Sri Shyama Lahiri Mahasaya:
Volume 2

Srimad Bhagavad Gita: Spiritual Commentaries by Yogiraj Sri Sri Shyama
Charan Lahiri Mahasay and Swami Sriyukteshvar Giri

A Collection of Biographies of 4 Kriya Yoga Gurus
by Swami Satyananda Giri

Kriya Yoga
by Sri Sailendra Bejoy Dasgupta

Paramhansa Swami Yogananda: Life-portrait and Reminiscences
by Sri Sailendra Bejoy Dasgupta

Yoni Tantra: Commentary on Selected Verses In Light of Kriya Yoga
by n.w. "kashi" ("bala gopee")

Breinigsville, PA USA
24 January 2010
231277BV00003B/36/P